THE
MUSIC
INDUSTRY

The practical guide to understanding the essentials

by
HENRI BIERMANS
DSS Publishing

Published by DSS Publishing
A division of Da Street Sound Limited
145-157 St. John Street (Level 2)
EC1V 4PY London
United Kingdom

Front and back cover and page design by DSS Publishing
Printed and bound: see last page for details

A catalogue record for this book is available from the British Library.

ISBN: 978-0-9555680-0-8

IMPORTANT

To Jacqueline, Henri,
Marjolein, Pamela, Stephan,
and Eva.

DSS Publishing

Contents

15

1
Introduction

WHO THIS BOOK IS FOR

If you are a musician, composer, lyricist, performing artist, or music professional looking for a concise, easy-to-read reference work on the music business, this book is for you. It addresses—in a nutshell—all relevant details of the industry by offering what you need to know and cutting out the rest.

UNDERSTANDING THE BASICS

The Music Industry: The Practical Guide to Understanding the Essentials is a collection of vital facts for those pursuing a career in the music industry with limited research time available. This book provides key pieces of information that have been gathered, summarized, structured, and put into context for easy comprehension.

To understand the business and its workings, you must first grasp the basics. My goal is to equip you with what you need to succeed, including:

- the basic structures of the music industry
- the workings, laws, and parties involved
- today's music market, including the online market
- how to protect your rights/copyright
- how and what royalties are distributed and collected by beneficiaries nationally and internationally

Should you already have taken the initial steps and need clear-cut advice on how to proceed, this manual will also benefit you. If you find yourself in the midst of record contract negotiations, are about to meet with a record label, producer, publisher, manager, lawyer, financier, agent, rep, or executive to discuss a cooperation, or are planning to release songs to the public independently by cooperating with national or international distributors or online music service providers, it covers all core elements, giving you a well-rounded understanding so that you can achieve your goals faster.

MARKETS ABROAD

This guide primarily discusses the players involved and the legal structures and regulations pertaining to music markets in the U.S. and the United Kingdom. However, differences relating to the Canadian, other European, and Asian markets are also spelled out, should they apply. Now that we've set our groundwork, let's get started.

2
Copyright

Author ▪ Work ▪ Copyright ▪ Owner of Copyright ▪ Basic Rights of Copyright ▪ Performing Rights

Basic Legal Terminology

Your first step is to familiarize yourself with the basic legal terminology frequently used in music contracts, which will build a foundation for succeeding chapters. We'll first define a number of commonly used terms: "author," "work," "copyright", and "ownership of copyright."

The Author

The author is the person, or group, who creates the original work (i.e., a composition or the corresponding lyrics to a composition). The term "author" can be substituted with the words songwriter, music creator, or composer. One who arranges a composition can also be an author. For reasons of simplicity, I will use the personal pronouns "he" "his" and "him" when referring to the author or artist in this guide.

The Work

The original work of authorship is defined as a distinctive, non-copied, intellectual creation of sufficient substance that meets minimal standards of originality. This includes musical, literary, artistic, and dramatic works, both published and unpublished. A composition, a sound recording, a sample, an arrangement, song lyrics, sheet music, or cover-related artwork for a record release are all examples of what constitutes a work.

Copyright

Copyright is a legal term that defines and protects the rights granted by law to the author of the original work, regardless of his nationality or domicile. No copyright registration is required to protect the creator of the work. It automatically exists when the author puts the original work in a tangible, fixed form of expression, as on a media from which it may be reproduced. Examples of physical media are CDs, DVDs, tapes, and sheet music.

Owner of Copyright in the Song

The author of the original work is the sole owner of copyright to the work he created. The author of the original work, defined here as a song consisting of music and lyrics, is the owner of:

- Copyright in the *literary* work (lyrics)
- Copyright in the *musical* work (composition)

Owner of Copyright in the Sound Recording

The author of the original work may also be the owner of:

- Copyright in the *sound recording*

This is the case if the author has recorded a performance of the work and saved the sound recording, also called master or master recording, on a physical media from which it may be reproduced. In this scenario, the author also acts as the recording/performing artist of his work. Should the author solely work as a songwriter for other performing artists and not be involved in performing, recording, producing, mastering, and financing of the sound recording, he is not copyright holder of the sound recording.

There is thus a commonly accepted rule in the music industry to bear in mind: the owner of copyright in the sound recording is generally the entity who *arranges* and *pays for* the sound recording to be made. This can, but does *not* necessarily have to be, the author of the work himself. It can also be, and often is, a record company, producer, or production company interested in exploiting the author's work commercially.

Author versus Performing Artist (Part 1)

Understanding the difference between the author, the performing artist, and the related rights each party holds is key to comprehending how the music industry functions. The financial aspect of royalty payments that each party is entitled to is another essential part of the industry. To help you navigate through the steps, Figure 1 gives a synopsis of the workings that will be explained in detail in subsequent chapters.

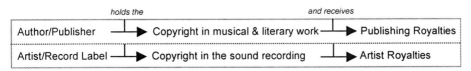

Figure 1.

Basic Rights of Copyright

The author of the original work is by rule the *first owner* of copyright and automatically holds certain basic yet *exclusive* rights in the work. This means that only the author is free to exercise these rights, and that other parties are prohibited from using the work without his consent.

The author can, however, grant certain—one or several—rights to another party. This is common practice if the author plans to market the work in return for payment. When an author generates revenue from his work, it's referred to as exploiting. Ownership of copyright in the work is then licensed or assigned to companies specializing in this trade. Examples of licensed groups include record labels, publishing companies, and production companies. Hence, only the author or those deriving their rights through the author can rightfully claim copyright.

Each national Copyright Act covers the copyright laws of that country. And each country has its own explicit definition of the basic rights of copyright as a part of its national copyright laws. Although copyright laws vary between countries, the basic protections are nearly identical. These are also the main rights that can be granted by the authors of a work to other parties. This is advantageous when dealing with international copyright issues and helps simplify and thus better understand the legal matters relating to copyright. I shall use the U.S. definition as an overall illustration.

In the United States, Section 106 of the 1976 Copyright Act defines the basic rights of copyright. In summary, it gives the owner of copyright the exclusive right to:

- **Reproduce** (Mechanical Right) the copyrighted work in various forms, such as a sound recording or printed publication
- **Prepare** derivative works, which are new versions based on the original work
- **Distribute** or issue copies or phonorecords of the copyrighted work to the public by sale or other transfer of ownership, such as rental, lease, or lending
- **Perform** (Performing Right or Public Performance Right) the copyrighted work publicly, such as playing the musical and literary work in public arenas, including pubs, jukebox, radio, television, nightclubs, live shows, and motion pictures

- **Display** the copyrighted work publicly, which applies to pictorial, graphic, or sculptural works
- In the case of sound recordings, perform the work publicly by means of a digital audio transmission

To put it all in context, this means that as an author these are *your* exclusive rights that apply once you have composed a new and original song and have documented and saved music and/or lyrics in a material form. This can either be in form of a sound recording of the music and vocals, a sound recording of the music, the lyrics in writing, or both music and lyrics in writing. The medium on which the music is saved can be sheet music on paper, lyrics saved on CD-ROM, or on any other form of media from which it can be read. You, the composer, have the right of "first use" of your work once it is created and saved. You can thus decide what to do or what not to do with your work. If you want to, you can put it in a drawer, lock it, and throw away the key forever. But you may also decide to grant rights to other companies in return for payment, typically the more popular option. The different sources of income are called royalties.

In the United Kingdom, Chapter II, section 16 et seqq of the 1988 Copyright, Designs and Patent Act (CDPA) provides the British definition of the basic rights of copyright.

Other countries such as Germany (as part of the 1965 Urheberrechtsgesetz), France, Japan, or Canada, to name a few, equally have their own definition as part of their copyright law. And obviously, the list does not end here. For the exact definition of the basic rights of copyright in your country, contact your national copyright or patent office. WIPO provides a comprehensive directory of the copyright, trademark, and patent offices covering 183 countries.

Putting copyrights aside for a moment, we're going to concentrate on the subject of "rights" and clarify several points that require further explanation.

Performing Rights
The term "performing rights" may cause some confusion, as it describes specific rights of both the author and the performing artist of a composition.

Definition

Performing rights define the basic rights that the *performing artists* hold in their performances and in the sound recordings of their performances. This term, however, should not be confused with the public performance rights that refer to an *author's* right to perform his works publicly that we looked at as part of the author's basic rights of copyright on the previous page.

The performing rights of artists are thus related, though not identical, to the basic rights of copyright in a work. In summary, they prevent other parties from[1]:

- broadcasting and recording their live performances
- copying, distributing, renting, and lending recordings of their performances
- broadcasting sound recordings to the public by electronic transmission, including on-demand services
- playing sound recordings of their performances in public

All rights are exclusively held by the performing artists unless granted to a third party by written consent. If the author of a song is equally the performing artist of the song, he is the owner of both rights.

Author versus Performing Artist (Part 2)

To better understand the difference between the author, the performing artist, and the rights each party holds, take a look at the outline below:

A Musician can be a		
Songwriter/Author *who is* Owner of Copyright in the Work (i.e., song, composition) *and holds the* Copyright in the Musical Work & Copyright in the Literary Work *including the Performing Rights as part of the Basic Rights of Copyright* *and may grant certain rights (Publishing Rights) in the work to*	and/or	Performing/Recording Artist *who is* Owner of the Performing Rights *and holds the* Rights in the Performance of a Work & Copyright in the Sound Recording, *but not the Performing Rights as part of the Basic Rights of Copyright* *and may grant certain rights (Rights in the Sound Recording) to* a Record Company
Royalty Collection Agencies · and/or · Publishing Companies		

Figure 2.

In wrapping up, if the author composes an original song, arranges and pays for the sound recording in which he is the sole performer in a studio, and equally performs his song in public, he is owner of copyright in the musical and literary work as well as owner of the performing rights. This includes the rights in the performance of the work and the copyright in the sound recording.

3
Granting Rights

Grant ▪ License ▪ Assign

Rights to use a work are shared with a third party through granting, licensing, or assigning of specific rights.

Grant
The term "grant" means to license or assign specific rights to other parties. As described in Chapter Two, the copyright owner of a work or sound recording can grant his copyright to entities such as record, production, and publishing companies, as well as royalty collecting societies.

License
When a copyright owner licenses—or grants a license of—the copyright in his work to another party, he does not surrender the underlying copyright for his work. The work itself is not transferred and the creator still owns the rights. You could compare it to the author lending his work out for a temporary period of time. Using legal terms, the copyright owner (licensor) signs a license agreement for a specified term with the licensee (other parties) during which the licensee has permission to exploit or administer the work. Note that copyright in a work is generally licensed to royalty collecting societies for a limited term not exceeding several years. The agreement can be cancelled thereafter without any further obligations to the licensor.

Assign
When a copyright owner assigns the rights of his work or sound recording to another party, he transfers, and thereafter no longer owns these rights. Assigning the rights restricts the creator from ownership of his work during the period of the contract. Using legal terminology, the copyright owner (assignor) signs an assignment agreement for a specified term with the assignee (other parties, such as the publisher or record label) who can then exploit the work. The term of an assignment is usually for the duration of copyright. Though the term of an assignment is generally longer than those of a license, it depends on the wording in the contract signed by both parties.

As an author or performing artist, think twice before assigning your rights to another party. A license agreement may be preferable since you typically give up less control for a shorter period of time.

4
Music Publishing

**Definition ▪ Publisher ▪ Author ▪
Record Label ▪ Publishing Rights**

Music publishing involves:

- Music Publishers promoting, marketing, and linking signed authors and their respective musical works with suitable recording artists for the purpose of having them recorded and released by the record label to which they are signed
- Placing musical works, unpublished or published according to the conditions specified in the publishing contract, composed by authors in other media, such as motion picture soundtracks, commercials, television broadcasts, and gaming machines
- Issuing licenses to licensees and handling copyright registration and administration with collecting societies for published songs
- Administering and supervising the collection and payment of publishing royalties to their writers and co-publishers
- Clearing sample usage

The ultimate goal of music publishing is to yield significant income through high volume sales and airplay generated from the commercial exploitation of the works.

Publisher

A music publisher exploits an author's musical and literary work, acts as an agent on behalf of the author, and focuses on the points listed above. Typically the terms of agreement and the publisher's responsibilities would be outlined in the contract. Some music publishers take the initiative to help authors fine-tune their writing skills by bringing together composers to collaborate on songwriting projects. Other publishers assist writers who record, release, and publicly perform their own songs in finding a record deal. A publisher may even sign a performing artist or band and invest in their creative development in return for a royalty share once they get signed to a record label. A royalty advance is often included as part of a publishing deal. If and when any of these possible scenarios materialize depends on the size and clout of the publishing company and the quality and marketability of the works. If the package is what Artist and Repertoire (A&R) Managers are looking for, a record label contract could soon be under way.

Publisher versus Author

Authors can venture on their own if they accumulate enough hit record releases through a prominent performing artist using their songs. It is not uncommon for authors with a successful track record to act as publishers themselves. They are no longer dependent on publishing companies to promote their works, as they have created sufficient demand for their works from preceding success stories. They directly collaborate with performing artists, record labels, production companies, or film studios seeking new material. This cuts out the publishing company as middleman. The author becomes his own publisher in this scenario.

Regarding authors who perform their own songs, they are not required to collaborate with publishers as they exploit their own musical and literary works. They would more likely join forces with record labels to help them successfully release and promote their works.

Publisher versus Record Label

In a nutshell, the publisher (also called the publishing side) assists and works for the author; the record label assists and works for the performing artist. Here's an example of how the author and publisher collaborate:

The Author *writes a*
Song *and grants copyright in his song to a*
Publisher *who markets the song, issues*
Licenses to licensees (song users), *and collects*
most Royalties in return, *which are split into the*
Publisher's share *that remains with the Publisher and*
Writer's share *that is paid out to the Author.*

Figure 3.

Publisher's share and writer's share are covered in the section titled "Author's and Publisher's Royalty Split" (see royalty split for more detailed information).

Publishing Rights (Overview)

A publisher of a musical composition with lyrics is the entity who holds the copyright to the musical and literary work. In general, this is either the author of the work himself, in case he publishes his song on his own, or a publishing company to whom the copyright has been granted.

The author generally grants the following rights of his song to a publishing company:

- Copyright in the literary work
- Copyright in the musical work

In doing so, the author grants the publishing company his:

- Performing rights
- Mechanical rights

Performing and mechanical rights, as we already learned, are part of the basic rights of copyright.

Publishing rights can be granted by the author of a work to the following agencies:

- Royalty collecting societies, also called royalty collection agencies or simply collecting societies
- Publishing companies

Publishing rights permit the publisher to promote the works in order to enhance exposure and get them licensed. This effectively produces sales. Together, all facets unite to push a marketing program to promote the work and enhance profits. The rights protect each entity, and all parts play a role in maintaining organization within the music industry.

5
Music Print Publishing

Definition ▪ Companies ▪ Copyright

Music print publishers specialize in selling printed music. Printed music consists of sheet music, scores, orchestrations, song folios, and lyric folios. Music print publishers authorize print-related usages such as photocopying, arranging, adapting, and reprinting lyrics. Revenues made through this type of publishing have decreased over the last decades due to dwindling popularity.

There are a small number of large firms that engage in this line of work, among them being Hal Leonard, the largest worldwide print publisher, based in the U.S., and Alfred Publishing, a publishing company that purchased the Warner Brother Publications division from Warner Music Group in 2005 (*http://www.alfred.com*). Hal Leonard represents, in print, some of the world's best known publishers, artists, and writers, including three of the four major music publishing firms: Sony/BMG, EMI, and Universal Publishing, along with the Famous Music Corporation, Chappell & Co, Lennon & McCartney, Peermusic, Elvis Presley Music, Really Useful Group (Andrew Lloyd Webber), Rodgers & Hammerstein, and others (*http://www.halleonard.com*). Music Sales Limited, a company based in the U.K., is currently one of Europe's largest music print publishers. Any publisher or author can market and sell his own works in printed form. However, this is not common practice. As a rule, this venture only makes sense if the song has been published or has been a commercial success, leading to an increased demand by customers. Consumers would be more interested in the sheet music of a major hit record or Broadway melody than an unknown song.

The copyright generally needs to be licensed in the form of a licensing agreement by the publisher to the print publisher, who commonly monitors, collects, and distributes the license fees to the publisher. Eventually the author's percentage of the fees trickles down from the publisher to the author.

Figure 4.

6
Publishing Rights and Royalties

Players ▪ Royalties ▪ Royalty Split ▪ International Publishing Income ▪ Artist versus Author's Royalties ▪ Co-writer's Credits

Authors, performing artists, record labels, and publishing companies at some point bring in income from their work. In this chapter, we will take an inside look at the music publishing income. These are the revenues that authors and publishing companies receive from exploiting copyrighted works commercially. We will examine who pays what, who gets what, and who collects and distributes the monies. We will also learn how performing rights and copyright are involved in the overall scheme, and who needs to transfer what rights to whom.

We will look at the players, define the terms "royalties" and "royalty collecting societies," and subsequently cover each of the publishing royalties in detail. We will also clarify existing legal and operational differences that pertain to publishing royalties by country (including the U.S., Canada, the U.K., and Europe as a whole). Artist royalties will be further discussed in a subsequent chapter. Now that you are familiar with copyrights and grants as defined in Chapters Two and Three, let's get to the part that peaks the most interest: the money aspect.

Players
The main players in the music industry are:
Author
Performer
Publisher
Record Company
Royalty Collecting Societies

Royalties
Definition
Royalties are license fees paid by the licensee—the person or entity who will exploit the work—to the owner or licensor of copyright for the exploitation of copyright.

Publishing Royalties

Publishing royalties can be broken down into primary and secondary publishing income (see Figure 4). The four major categories that fit into primary and secondary publishing income are: mechanical rights and performance rights, which are part of primary income. Synchronization and print belong to secondary income. Both primary and secondary income can be major sources of income for an artist. Other revenues such as DART monies and translation and adaptation also belong to secondary publishing income sources.

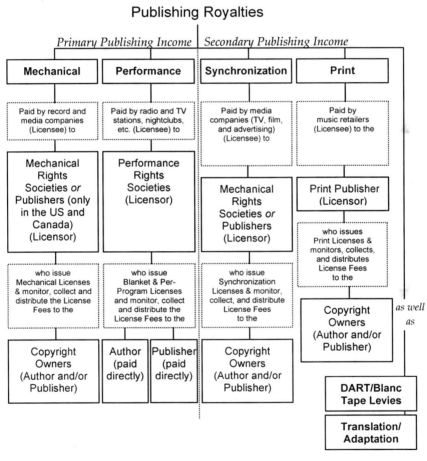

Figure 5.

License and Royalty Administration

License and royalty administration includes negotiating agreements with and issuing licenses to licensees, as well as collecting, monitoring, and distributing the related license fees paid by the licensees to the copyright owners.

Author's and Publisher's Royalty Split
Traditionally, when authors collaborate with publishing companies, the publishing royalties collected (including mechanical, public performance, and synchronization royalties) are split 50/50. Half goes to the publishing company as payment for their services and half goes to the author. The collecting society's commission, should the publisher be affiliated with one, is deducted prior to splitting the monies. It is more and more common, especially in European countries, to allocate a higher percentage of income to the songwriter. A 75/25, 70/30[2], or 60/40 percent royalty split in favor of the writer is viable and the present going rate for new songwriters. Contracts with these splits do exist in growing numbers. The writer/publisher royalty split is specified in every publishing contract.

The following is a brief example of how the monies could be distributed: a song is written by two authors, of whom writer one is a member of ASCAP and writer two a member of BMI. The writer's split in this song is 30/70: thirty percent is designated to writer one and seventy percent goes to writer two. If the writer/publisher split is 60/40, and one dollar of gross revenue is to be split between the three parties, then the publisher gets 40 cents (1 x 40% = 0.40), writer one gets 18 cents (1.00 - 0.40 = 0.60 · 0.60 x 30% = 0.18), and writer two gets 42 cents (0.60 x 70% = 0.42). The clearance form (see Chapter Nine, section "Clearance Forms" for more on clearance forms) that is submitted by the publishing company to ASCAP and BMI should indicate these splits as such. If two publishers were involved, then the 40% publisher's share would be split between both publishers at the ratio agreed upon by both parties.

International Publishing Income
Publishing companies collaborate internationally through a network of national publishing companies, also called sub-publishers. It is important to note that international publishing income distributed by publishing companies should always be computed "at source." That is, the revenues paid out to the authors must be computed from *all* monies earned in the foreign country without any prior deductions by other parties. This should be clearly stipulated in publishing or sub-publishing contracts. Should the sub-publisher be part of the same holding company as the publisher, no additional commission should be retained by the sub-publisher. A sub-publisher may charge up to

25% of national gross revenues collected, though 10–15% is more common. The total share charged by publishing firms both domestic and foreign should not exceed 50%. Royalty collection societies collect and distribute cross-border royalties worldwide for less than 25%, which is a lot, so publishing companies charging double the rate are pricey. Publishing companies, on the other hand, do more than just monitor and collect money, so one can argue that they earn their keep.

Writer's Split
The writer's split is the division of the writer's share of royalties between the authors who collaborate on writing a song. If a lyricist and a composer participate in writing a song, royalties are generally split 50/50 between both parties. Both sides can, however, agree on a different writer's split, such as 60/40 or 20/80 corresponding to each side's contribution. The writer's split is thus negotiable. It is best to agree on the writer's split ahead of time. When writing a song in a team, the copyright in the musical and literary work are shared by all writers and therefore cannot be licensed exclusively.

Artist Royalties versus Author's Royalties
Although the author and performing artist may be the same person, they legally remain two distinct entities and receive different royalty payments by different royalty collecting societies. Publishing royalties include the author's royalties. The artist's royalties are, in contrast, not part of the publishing royalties. Depending on the contractual terms of an agreement and the type of deal signed between the parties, an author can sign to a record label as a performing artist and at the same time to a publishing company as an author who writes songs for other performing artists. Record labels typically frown on such agreements.

Royalties (Co-writer's Credits)
Recording artists or managers occasionally request a co-writer's credit on a song, thus sharing in both the artist and publishing royalties. In exchange, the producers push the song into the media by adding it to their repertoire, particularly if the writer is not well-known.[3] This practice should in general not be tolerated by authors if they have developed and composed a work on their own. Deciding on whether a contribution merits a credit is an area that is not as clear cut and from time to time leads to disputes between producers and writers.

7
Royalty Collecting Societies

**Definition ▪ Types ▪ Membership ▪ Foreign Royalties ▪
Commission Rates ▪ Private Licensing Companies ▪ Song
Research Services ▪ ISWC**

Publishing licenses and royalties are administered either via royalty collecting societies or via internal royalty administration departments of publishing companies.

Royalty collecting societies (RCSs) are predominantly non-profit, though at times for-profit, entities. Most of them are government owned organizations that act as exclusive agents on behalf of the members, who are the authors and publishers. They provide clearance, licensing, and royalty accounting services pertaining to musical works in exchange for a commission rate. The commission is a percentage of the revenues collected. Hence, the RCSs earn a commission for the services they provide. RCSs generally operate through reciprocal collection agreements with one another to collect and distribute royalties in and to foreign territories. They also audit record companies.

Types of Collecting Societies
The royalty collecting societies responsible for administering publishing income for authors and publishing companies are the

- Mechanical Rights Societies
- Performing Rights Societies

They cover primary publishing income as well as certain secondary publishing income. They also perform varied tasks, which are explained in subsequent chapters. (See Figure 5, Chapter 6 for a graphic representation.)

BIEM is the umbrella organization representing more than forty mechanical rights societies in over forty countries. CISAC is the umbrella organization representing the performance rights societies worldwide.

Members
Next to authors, publishing companies that want to rid themselves from their licensing and royalty administration tasks can equally affiliate with RCSs.

Membership Requirements
Membership eligibility requirements and fees for authors and publishing companies who want to join vary from collecting society to collecting society. Some charge a one-time admission fee and an annual membership fee, while others waive the latter. For writers who wish to affiliate with a society, evidence of a public performance, broadcast, or a commercially recorded or published record of at least one composition may be required. For publishers who apply for membership, evidence of legitimate music publishing activities may be required. This is usually satisfied by proof of ownership or control of the publishing rights in relation to a number of commercially recorded and released compositions. However, not all societies have these requirements. Contact the national society of your choice for exact details.

Membership Restrictions
There is one restraint to be aware of. Depending on the rules and regulations set out by a number of societies, an author may only be able to sign up for membership to *one* mechanical rights society only. The society the author selects will administer all mechanical licenses on a worldwide basis. This does not apply to performing rights societies.

Reciprocal Agreements
RCSs collaborate cross-border through reciprocal agreements, thus establishing a worldwide network of like-minded organizations that assist in administering and controlling the worldwide use of musical and literary works. Among their tasks are collecting and distributing related royalties for authors and publishers in foreign territories.

Foreign Royalty Collecting Societies
You do not always have to affiliate with a collecting society in your country of residence or the country where your publishing company or record label is registered. This primarily depends on the rules set out by each collecting society. Performing rights and broadcasting societies are less restrictive. For instance, you can live in France and affiliate with a mechanical rights society in Britain. Or register your publishing company in Britain and sign up for membership as a

publishing company with a performing rights society in the U.S. Membership requirements are commonly summarized on the Web sites of each society. Check the FAQ section on the Web site first, or contact them by phone or email. A complete list of collecting societies arranged by category and country is provided in Chapter Twenty-seven. Links to the Web site addresses of each society (if available) are included.

Collecting and Distributing Foreign Royalties

Royalty collecting societies administer international licenses and collect and distribute royalties on a national basis per country, per song. The monies are distributed to the societies abroad with whom the beneficiaries are affiliated. These organizations will then directly pay out the monies to the beneficiaries. A commission is charged by both societies for the services they render. National laws frequently prohibit local collecting societies to directly distribute monies to publishers that are located abroad. Large publishing companies also use a network of local sub-publishers to collect and distribute monies internationally. As is explained in Chapter Nine, public performance royalties are generally not collected on a per song basis.

Commission Rates

The aggregate commission rate charged by both foreign and domestic royalty collecting societies for administering international licenses and collecting and distributing related royalties is generally between 10 and 22% of total revenues earned.

Term for Collecting Foreign Royalties

The process of monitoring, collecting, distributing, and paying out foreign license fees may take between twelve and eighteen months.

Private Licensing Companies

Music copyright research, clearance, licensing, and royalty accounting services to licensees are also provided by privately run organizations. Critics of national collecting societies have pointed to the incomprehensibility of the payment schemes used to account for and calculate license fees, the inefficiency of accurately monitoring the usage, the elevated cost of operating their services, and the financial muscle they use to stay in control with helpful industry connections and lobbying factions in the right places. Private organizations are emerging to make up for some of the shortcomings. Whether they can assist songwriters more effectively at a lower cost and beyond national borders remains to be seen. For now, no real substitute for national societies is available, as they only offer partial licensing and/or monitoring services for their clients.

- MRI (*http://www.musicreports.com*)
- SoundExchange (*http://www.soundexchange.com*)
- Nielsen SoundScan (*http://www.soundscan.com*)

The previous list shows three independently run companies. MRI is an independent administrator of music rights in the television industry and has developed proprietary databases and systems to administer ASCAP and BMI "Per Program" licenses. SoundExchange focuses on public performance rights in sound recordings for particular digital and satellite transmissions. Soundscan is an information system that tracks sales of music and music video products throughout the United States and Canada, though it does not collect and distribute license fees. Check The Yomuse Music Directory, also labeled The Music Directory in this guide, online for further companies. It is located at *http://www.yomuse.com/musdir/index.htm*.

Song Research Services
To track down the owners of musical copyrights or licensing details of a particular song or melody, the following informational sources may be of use:

- Royalty Collecting Societies have vast catalogs representing millions of songs and melodies by their members in every form and style, including rock, pop, country, gospel, TV and film music, jazz, Latin, big band music, and others. The largest collecting societies, based on number of compositions held in their repertoire, provide extensive online song indexes that enable users to search for a song by title and find the name of the corresponding author, publisher, and recording artist. The database also lists the originating royalty collecting society and territory. A query for songs by author, performer, work number assigned by the societies, or International Standard Musical Work Code (ISWC) may also be possible. Here are several online song index search services that could lend a helping hand:

    - ASCAP Clearance Express (ACE) (*http://www.ascap.com/ace*
    - BMI Hyper Repertoire databank *http://repertoire.bmi.com*

- HFA Songfile
  http://www.harryfox.com/public/songfile.jsp
- GEMA (German Mechanical Rights Society)
  http://www.gema.de/engl/musicsearch (in German)
- SACEM (French Mechanical Rights Society)
  http://www.sacem.fr/catel/fwk/main.jsp
- MCPS Alliance Online Services (registration required)
  http://www.mcps-prs-alliance.co.uk/allianceonline

- You can also check the U.S. Copyright Office by going online at *http://www.copyright.gov/records/cohm.html* and entering either the name of the author, title, registration number, or perform a combined search. For more details, refer to Circular 22, "How to Investigate the Copyright Status of a Work," published by the U.S. Copyright Office.
- Professional research companies also perform copyright search services, although they are not free of charge. A list of companies is supplied in The Music Directory.
- Trade publications can also be examined. Billboard and CMJ are the most well-know in the U.S. A list of online trade publications categorized by country is also provided in The Music Directory.

ISWC

The ISWC (International Standard Musical Work Code) is a unique, permanent, and internationally recognized reference number for the identification of intellectual property, such as musical and literary works, that are within repertoires controlled by members of CISAC. The code is allocated and administered by the International ISWC Agency. The ISWC is part of the Common Information System (CIS) plan set up by CISAC. The ISWC Agency is appointed by the ISO, the International Organization for Standardization. Their Web page can be accessed at *http://www.iswc.org.*

The ISWC should not be confused with the International Standard Recording Code (ISRC), which is allocated by IFPI. IFPI is an agency that is equally appointed by the ISO.

8
Mechanical Rights and Royalties

Definition ▪ Societies ▪ Licensees, Licenses, Fees ▪ Licensing Services ▪ Membership ▪ Royalty Collection and Distribution ▪ Commission ▪ Royalty Rate ▪ Statutory Rate ▪ BIEM

Mechanical royalties are compulsory license fees that, as determined by copyright law, must be paid by the licensee to the copyright owner for the right to use a composition. This can involve "mechanically," electro-magnetically, or digitally manufacturing and reproducing the work for public distribution. A mechanical license fee needs to be paid for each record or song that is manufactured and distributed.

Mechanical Right
The term "mechanical right" dates back to the time when all reproductions of music were carried out by mechanical processes. Even though reproductions nowadays are carried out in a variety of electronic and digital ways, the term "mechanicals" has become enshrined into industry jargon.[4]

Mechanical Rights Societies
A mechanical rights society (MRS) administers mechanical licenses and royalties, along with others, on behalf of its members, the copyright owners, in exchange for a percentage of the revenues collected.

Here is a list of some of the largest MRSs worldwide:

- SDRM (France);
- MCPS (United Kingdom);
- AMCOS (Australia);
- NCB (Denmark);
- STEMRA (Netherlands);
- SARRAL (South Africa);
- HFA (USA);
- GEMA (Germany);
- JASRAC (Japan).

The first five societies cited also administer mechanical licenses and royalties, in cooperation with respective national societies to aid cost savings and effective administration, in countries sharing historical ties. For example, if the country was a former colony in the past, they would have historical ties. A list stipulating what collecting society administers what territories is provided in the back of this guide.

Copyright Owner

The copyright owner is either the author of the work or the publishing company to whom the copyright of the work has been granted. Should the latter hold true, the mechanical royalties are commonly split evenly or unevenly, depending on the contractual agreement between the author and publisher.

Licensor

The licensor is the party that negotiates agreements and issues licenses to the licensees. This is either a MRS or the publishing company. The author does not commonly act as licensor himself. This is above all due to the lack of know-how on how much to charge for different licenses, how to negotiate a deal, as well as the lack of time and contacts in the music publishing industry that are necessary to work out national and cross-boarder publishing issues.

License Fees

Depending on the agreement, license fees must be paid by the licensee to the licensor up-front on the number of records or copies of songs to be manufactured when submitting the license application. Another alternative is to pay periodically—usually quarterly—on the number of records or copies of songs sold or distributed during this period.

Licensees

The licensees are record, media, film, and advertising companies who record, distribute, and broadcast products containing copyright protected musical works. Examples of such products are records in any format (e.g., as CDs, LPs, tapes, MDs, Vinyl, etc.) and piano rolls. They also include TV and radio programs, commercials, and feature films. We shall look at these products and how they relate to MRSs in more detail in consequent chapters.

Licensing Agreement

The rights granted to the licensee, the term the rights are granted for, the method of computing the royalties to be paid by the licensee, and the time or conditions when payments become due are set out in a contractual agreement, also called a licensing agreement or license.

Collecting and Distributing Mechanical Royalties
The publisher is either paid by the licensee directly or via the mechanical rights societies indirectly, which is prevalent in countries other than the U.S. and Canada. In the first scenario, the publisher directly issues and negotiates a license with and receives payment from the licensee. The mechanical rights society is not involved in this transaction.

For mechanical licenses that are issued by the mechanical rights society on behalf of the publisher, the former will act as middleman and take care of the administrative tasks just described in exchange for a commission charged. After receiving the mechanicals, the publisher will then pay out the writer's share of royalties to the author.

Mechanical rights societies may alternatively pay out the writer's share directly to the author, which again is more widespread in countries other than the U.S. and Canada. As you can see, there are a variety of ways mechanical royalties reach their beneficiaries:

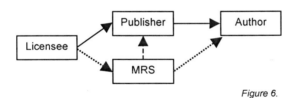

Figure 6.

Types of Licenses
License fees and commission rates vary depending on the licensee's business. The licensee can use musical works in a variety of ways:

- As title song or background music in motion picture films, home videos or DVDs, or television programs such as sitcoms or TV films. These are called synchronization licenses.
- In drama productions, midi, karaoke and backing track products, interactive games or gaming machines, telephone services, video jukebox machines, off-air recordings of radio and television broadcasts made by educational establishments, in-flight audio systems, religious-based services, novelties, mobile phone ringtones and ringbacks, and so on.

Mechanical rights societies have catalogued these different usages in "licensing schemes," "licensing categories," or "license types." Each scheme provides information regarding the license, the standard license fees and commission rates to be paid by the licensees, the nature of exploitation stipulating what the license allows the user to do and how the music is exploited, special restrictions, and further details regarding the terms of payment and distribution. The type of contract signed between the licensee and the collecting society may equally have a bearing on the license fees and commission rates. Discounted fees and rates are often granted to licensees. So there is some room for negotiation. The size and clout of an organization may be beneficial when trying to get a more favorable deal. A more favorable deal for the licensee is, however, not necessarily a more favorable deal for the beneficiaries. Lower royalties mean less money in the songwriter's pocket. To obtain a mechanical license, contact the local national MRS. This should be the country where you intend to reproduce the record.

Licensing Services
MRSs do not only administer mechanical licenses. They are overall responsible for the following licensing services, although exceptions do apply by country:

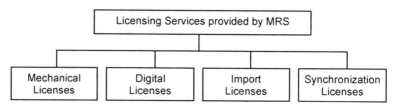

Figure 7.

Import licenses are required in order for the licensee to lawfully import records from the country of manufacturing into the country of destination. The licensee must, in addition to obtaining the mechanical license, obtain an Importation Request Form and complete and return it to the MRS.

Let's now look at the differences between the mechanical rights societies in the U.S. and Canada versus other countries around the world. In brief, we can say that the royalty computation and administration differ between countries.

Mechanical Rights Societies in the U.S.
The Harry Fox Agency (HFA) is the main MRS in the U.S. It offers mechanical, digital, and importation licensing services, though since 2002 no longer administers synchronization licenses. Mechanical licenses are only available to U.S. manufacturers or importers with a U.S. address. HFA issues licenses for products manufactured and distributed in the U.S. only. HFA also provides collection and monitoring services to its publisher clients for music distributed and sold in over ninety territories around the world through reciprocal agreements with mechanical rights organizations in those territories.

The current commission rate it charges for its services is 6.75% of royalties distributed. The current admission fee for a publishing company is $150 and the annual membership fee is $100. The present admission fee for an author is $75 and the annual membership fee is $50.

Membership admission requires anyone seeking to become an HFA affiliate publisher must have at least one song available for licensing through HFA and at least one song has to have been commercially released by a third party within the last twelve months prior to applying. For further information, go online and visit the Harry Fox Web site at *http://www.harryfox.com*. You will find details regarding the current statutory mechanical rate, the licenses they issue and forms to fill out, the online licensing facilities (HFA Songfile and HFA eMechanical), license fees charged, the term and method of distributing royalties, and more.

Mechanical Royalty Computation in the U.S.
Statutory Rate: A record company interested in using a song in a record is required to pay the U.S. copyright owner a per-song license fee, called the statutory rate, on all records it manufactures and distributes in the U.S. The statutory rate is ultimately set by the Librarian of Congress and the Copyright Office, in collaboration with the Copyright Arbitration Royalty Panel (CARP). The rate is adjusted from time to time resulting from economic changes that are in part based on the Consumer Price Index. As of January 1, 2006 the statutory rate for a song lasting five minutes or less is 9.1¢. For a song lasting in excess of five minutes, the statutory rate is 1.75¢ per minute. Thus, for a song lasting six minutes, the royalty is 6 x 1.75¢; for a song lasting seven minutes or less, the royalty is 7 x 1.75¢; and so on. To give an example: Should a record company publicly distribute 100 records containing three songs that each lasts less

than five minutes, it would have to pay a total mechanical royalty of $27.30 (statutory rate per song 9.1¢ x number of records 100 x number of songs on records 3) to either the publisher or the mechanical rights society.

Reduced Statutory Rate: Although the payment of mechanicals is legally required in the U.S., the statutory rate is negotiable. Record companies are therefore *not* obligated to pay the full statutory rate if they can convince the copyright owners to accept a reduced rate: 75% (3/4) of the statutory rate is not uncommon in the U.S. music industry. Whether record companies succeed in reducing the statutory rate depends on their negotiation skills and a variety of other factors. It obviously reduces the mechanical royalties paid to copyright owners. See Chapter Sixteen for related information on the controlled composition clause.

Mechanical Rights Society in Canada
The Canadian Musical Reproduction Rights Agency (CMRRA) is the largest mechanical rights society in Canada. It currently charges 6% of gross revenues collected for its services. There is no admission fee, nor is there an annual membership fee. Visit their Web site at http://www.cmrra.ca for membership requirements and additional information.

Mechanical Royalty Computation in Canada
Canada does *not* have a compulsory statutory rate comparable to the U.S. A per-song industry royalty rate based on a contractual agreement between the Canadian Record Company Association (CRCA) and major publishers is applied. CMRRA issues licenses under two plans: the Mechanical Licensing Agreement and "pay-as-you-press." According to the "pay-as-you-press" plan, the current royalty rate is 7.7¢ (Canadian currency) per copy manufactured for a song lasting five minutes or less, and 1.54¢ for each additional minute or fraction of a minute. For a song lasting 6.5 minutes, the total royalty would therefore be 10.78¢ (7.7¢ + 1.54¢ + 1.54¢). The industry royalty rate equally gets adjusted for inflation from time to time. Detailed information on mechanical and other licensing services is provided on the CMRRA Web site in a well structured and easy to read document named "CMRRA—Pay as you press." It can be accessed online at *http://www.cmrra.ca/cmrradocs/paypdocs.pdf*.

Mechanical Rights Societies in other Countries
In countries other than the U.S. and Canada, mechanical licenses

and royalties are only administered by mechanical rights societies and *not* by publishing companies. Mechanicals for each copy of a record manufactured, imported, and distributed in a country must first be paid by the licensees to the mechanical rights society of that country, which will then issue licenses. The MRS will pay out the revenues to the copyright owner, including the publisher and author, according to a set schedule and after deducting the commission.

Mechanical Royalty Computation in other Countries

Mechanical license fees are not issued on a per-song basis, as is common in the U.S. and Canada, but rather as a percentage of a record's published price to dealer (PPD), which is equal to the record's wholesale price. Alternatively, they are issued as a percentage of a record's retail price. The number of songs on a record is of no relevancy in computing the mechanical royalty. This procedure also applies to countries that are part of the European Union.

Mechanical Rights Society in the United Kingdom

The Mechanical Copyright Protection Society (MCPS) is the only mechanical rights collection society in the U.K. A one-time admission fee for publishers of $75 (£50) is charged when signing up for membership. MCPS levies and deducts a commission that ranges from 6.25% to 12.5%, depending on the licensing scheme signed, on the revenues collected for its services rendered. New members are frequently placed on the MCPS licensing scheme "AP2," whereby license fees must be paid up-front and the commission rate deducted by MCPS is 8.5% of PPD.

The licensing agreements and license schemes are summarized in a document called "Licensing Scheme Table Complete" found on the MCPS Internet site at *http://www.mcps.co.uk*. More information is also available online. It is interesting to note that if the record label, author, and publisher are one and the same person, then MCPS will waive the 8.5% commission rate, giving an exemption from mechanical royalty payment. An allowance is granted for promotional copies of the recording. All promotional copies must be prominently marked. MCPS equally offers a service called "Pan-European Licensing," a one-stop shop for clearing mechanical *and* performing rights in registered music across Europe for online and mobile usage for a 15% commission charge. Information can be found online at *http://www.mcps-prs-alliance.co.uk/licensingthefuture*. This may be of interest to those seeking to simplify licensing of their works across Europe.

Mechanical Royalty Computation in the United Kingdom

The license fee payable by users of copyrighted material for a record (e.g., CD, LP, MD, etc.) intended for retail sale to the public is 8.5% of the published price to dealer (PPD), exclusive of VAT (Value Added Tax or Sales Tax). If there is no PPD available, the royalty is 6.5% of the retail price, again exclusive of VAT.

BIEM

BIEM[5] is the Bureau International des Sociétés Gérant les Droits d'Enregistrement et de Reproduction Mécanique. It is the international organization representing many of the national mechanical rights societies. BIEM currently represents 45 societies from 43 countries. Member societies of BIEM enter into reciprocal agreements to allow each of them to represent the others' repertoire of protected works, the rights of which are granted to them by the composers, authors, and publishers affiliated with the national societies. In this way, a BIEM member society is able to license users for the vast majority of songs in the world. BIEM's role is to assist in collaboration between its member societies and to help solve problems that arise between individual members and between members and user groups. BIEM represents and defends the interests of its member societies, particularly in forums relating to authors' rights, such as WIPO, UNESCO, TRIPS (*http://www.wto.org*), and the WCO (*http://www.wcoipr.org*). BIEM negotiates a Standard Agreement with representatives of the International Federation of the Phonographic Industry (IFPI), thus fixing the conditions for the use of the repertoire of the societies by record producers. The Standard Agreement is applied by the member societies to the extent that there is no compulsory license or statutory license in their territory.

Royalty Rate

The royalty rate agreed between BIEM and IFPI is 11% on the Published Price to Dealers (PPD) and concerns physical audio products only. The PPD is the highest price charged by a record producer to retailers selling directly to consumers. Two deductions are applied on the gross royalty rate: 9% for rebates and discounts and 10% for packaging costs. This results in an effective rate of 9.009% of PPD. Rates for audio-visual use of protected works are negotiated on a territory by territory basis, as are rates for Internet and other usage.

Minimum Royalty Rate
The Standard Contract provides for a minimum royalty equal to two thirds of the normal royalty rate. There is also provision for a minimum budget royalty equal to 57% of the normal minimum royalty and concerns only re-releases of carriers not less than one year after the original release, priced at least 35% below the original price.

Standard Contract
The Standard Contract is a worldwide contract. Through their membership to BIEM societies are bound to enforce the Standard Contract in their respective territories of exploitation, but only to the extent that there are no statutory or compulsory provisions in force. For example, countries such as the U.S., the U.K., and Australia all have compulsory licensing provisions in their Copyright Law and various national methods of setting the applicable rate. The Standard Contract, however, expired on June 30, 2000. Negotiations on a new Standard Contract are not yet finalized. Societies and record producers are still operating under the provisions of the most recent version of the Standard Contract.

BIEM Contact
The General Secretariat of BIEM is based in Neuilly-sur-Seine, France. The Asia Pacific Regional Office is based in Singapore. The Central & Eastern European Regional Office is based in Budapest, Hungary. For further information, visit the BIEM Web site at *http://www.biem.org* or, should you have any questions, send a message to *info@biem.org*. This information was directly retrieved from the BIEM Web site.

9
Performance Rights and Royalties

**Definition ▪ Societies ▪ Commission Rates ▪
Licensees ▪ Blanket Licenses ▪ Membership ▪ Clearance Forms ▪
Royalty Allocation and Distribution**

Performance Royalties, also known as public performance royalties, are compulsory license fees paid by the licensees to the copyright owner for a public performance license. This license grants the right to play, perform, or broadcast a non-dramatic composition in public.

Performing Rights Societies
A performing rights society, also called performing rights organization or PRO, acts as a licensor and administers public performance licenses and royalties on behalf of the copyright owners in exchange for a percentage of the revenues collected from the exploitation of musical and literary works. The largest PROs in the U.S. are ASCAP, BMI, and SESAC. Outside the U.S., each country has at least one national PRO. The PROs collaborate cross-border through bilateral agreements. Here are some of the largest PROs worldwide:

- SACEM (France)
- PRS (United Kingdom)
- APRA (Australia)
- BUMA (Netherlands)
- SAMRO (South Africa)
- GEMA (Germany)
- JASRAC (Japan)

The first five societies cited above also administer the performance licenses and royalties, in cooperation with each respective national society for reasons of cost savings and for more effective and reliable administration, for countries sharing historical ties. A list of collecting societies and their Web sites are categorized by country in the back of this guide.

Public performance license fees earned from the exploitation of works in countries abroad are monitored and collected by each foreign PRO and distributed to the domestic performing rights society the authors and publishers are affiliated with. The foreign PRO will remit the author's share of revenues earned directly to the author's performing rights society after deducting a service fee, which will then pay out the remainder to the member.

Commission Rates
The commission rates vary, though on average runs between 6% and 15% of gross revenues collected.

Licensees
The licensees are the users who play, perform, or broadcast a composition in public. Examples are radio stations, television channels, nightclubs, restaurants, bars, grills, concerts, baseball and soccer stadiums, and amusement parks.

Licenses
A public performance license typically comes in form of a blanket license. This gives the licensee the right to publicly play, perform, or broadcast——without limiting the number of plays——every composition contained in the PROs repertoire for a contractual period of time in exchange for a profit participation in the licensee's revenues.

Blanket licenses are said to be used because it is near to impossible for any single entity to monitor each public performance on a case by case basis. The British performance rights society, PRS (Publishing Royalty Services), estimates the number of public performances per year at eight billion in the United Kingdom only. Monitoring each and every song, inputting the data into computers, and administering the licenses would be too big a task. The blanket license system is thus used in most countries around the world. Blanket licenses differ according to the license scheme and category of the public performance selected. Nightclubs, pubs, restaurants, bars, bowling venues, recreational parks, spas, shops, hairdressers, concert halls, television networks, radio stations, satellite and cable broadcasters, and video companies each fall into a different license scheme and are charged differently for their particular usage. The scale of fees varies greatly and ranges from several hundred to hundreds of thousands of dollars per license per year. Licenses for television networks can generate high public performance revenues. Individual "per program" public performance licenses may also be available to users who prefer to use specific recordings in their broadcast or public performance. However, not all government-run PROs issue individual licenses. Contact the PRO of your choice to for further details.

Motion Picture Performance Royalties

Public performance royalties for music used in motion pictures that are distributed and shown in movie theatres throughout the United States are not endorsed and thus not collected and distributed by PROs. In countries outside the U.S., this is not the case. Motion picture license fees are based on the percentage of box office receipts or on the number of seats or screenings per week. They are collected by local PROs and dispensed to the respective authors and publishers. U.S. based authors and publishers are equally entitled to this type of foreign income.

Membership

Both authors and publishers can sign up for membership for a set term, usually between two and three years. A one-off admission fee is generally charged. As a rule, authors pay less than publishing companies. Admission fees vary, though range from $100 for authors to $650 for publishers. An annual membership fee is not required by most performing rights societies. In case it is, the fee will normally be deducted from the royalties that are due to the copyright holders. When signing up, you grant the society the right to administer the public performance licenses on your behalf and collect and pay out the relevant royalties to you.

Membership for Authors

Authors can only sign up for membership with one collecting society per country. Some collecting societies even insist on administering the mechanical and performing rights and royalties for their members on a worldwide basis. Authors who affiliate with GEMA, for example, cannot affiliate with any other collecting society worldwide. Thus you cannot affiliate with PRS and MCPS as an author in the United Kingdom and with GEMA in Germany. Every collecting society has its internal policies on what a member can and cannot do. These policies vary. When you sign up as an author, you will have to decide if the collecting society will administer your royalties on a worldwide basis, or, providing this is an option, if you want to limit their administrative ability to specific territories. Signing up with several societies has its drawbacks as you have more administrative tasks to deal with, additional admission fees, and possibly membership fees to take into account. On the other hand, no additional charges are deducted from gross revenues by foreign collecting societies if you directly affiliate with local societies. Also, the domestic royalty pay-out time will not be delayed since no other societies are involved in the transaction.

Membership Requirements
Membership requirements vary. Some PROs have them, others don't. Certain PROs require authors to have a work that has been broadcast, performed live, and publishers to have contracts with authors covering a minimum number of works. Check with the admissions department to find out. It makes sense for an author to sign up only if a release of his work is imminent before registering.

Clearance Forms
After joining a PRO, the publisher submits a clearance form including relevant data such as title, authors, and publishers of songs controlled by him to the PRO. The songs will then be added to the PRO's master repertoire list.

Royalty Payment
Public performance royalties are paid out by PROs to the authors and publishers directly, though independently of each other.

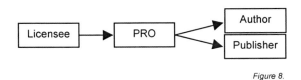

Figure 8.

Publishing Deal
At times, the publisher directly issues and negotiates a public performance license with and receives payment from the licensee. The PRO is not involved in this transaction. The author will then receive payment of his share of revenue from the publisher. This practice is not common with regards to public performance licenses.

Foreign Publishing Deal
Should the author enter into a publishing deal for representation in foreign countries and thereby assign his performing rights to a publisher who is affiliated with a collecting rights society, the international rights society will collect the license fees and distribute them to the local sub-publisher it has an agreement with. The author will thus not directly get paid by the PRO but by the publisher. He should therefore review a contract carefully for details on what rights

he assigns to whom and how monies are paid out prior to signing it. The music publisher normally allows its representative in each foreign territory to directly collect its share in the local country. (Also see International Publishing Income in Chapter Six for more information.)

Allocating Performance Royalties

PROs employ a variety of techniques to estimate how much to pay each member. They use census performance data supplied by major media research firms, sample performance data, airplay information listed on log sheets provided by radio stations, broadcast and cable TV performance data provided on cue-sheets by television networks, producers of syndicated programs, and motion pictures. Usage weightings are used as a means to assign a monetary value to music performances in broadcast media. These weightings are allocated by usage categories, including feature performances, themes, background, and commercials. Set lists provided by concert venues, artists, and bands that perform their songs live in public are also taken into account. Muzak provides PROs in the U.S. with performance data on fine music that is played in waiting rooms, grocery stores, and elevators. Each performing rights society applies and uses these techniques to a different degree. The title of a song, the respective writer and/or publisher, the length of airing, and the type of use are important details that are submitted to PROs.

Performing Rights Societies by Country
In the United States

The three main performing rights societies in U.S. are BMI (Broadcast Music Inc.), ASCAP (American Society of Composers, Authors and Publishers), and SESAC. The latter is a privately owned, for-profit company that covers between 1% and 3% of the performing rights administered. ASCAP and BMI are non-profit organizations that split the rest of the remaining performing rights, each covering by and large half of the remaining market.

In Canada

Society of Composers, Authors, and Music Publishers of Canada (SOCAN) is the organization that monitors, collects, and distributes performance royalties in the Canada.

In the United Kingdom

The Performing Rights Society (PRS) is the only organization that monitors, collects, and distributes performance royalties for authors and publishers in the U.K. PRS and MCPS have formed an operational alliance to improve the collaboration between both societies. The Mechanical-Copyright Protection Society (MCPS) is, however, a separate organization in terms of membership and the rights it licenses.

Performing Rights Societies in Germany

GEMA (Gesellschaft für musikalische Aufführungs- und Mechanische Vervielfältigungsrechte) is the only collecting society in Germany responsible for administering *both* public performance and mechanical licenses and royalties. In the U.K. the equivalent of GEMA is PRS *and* MCPS; in the U.S. the equivalent is one of following, BMI, ASCAP, or SESAC, *and* the Harry Fox Agency.

Other Performing Rights Societies

A list of MRSs and PROs categorized by country is provided in the end of this book. Web site addresses are equally listed.

Further Reading

For additional reading on how U.S. performing societies function, read through the article "The Operating Dynamics Behind ASCAP, BMI and SESAC, The U.S. Performing Rights Societies" by Barry M. Massarsky. The article is currently accessible online at *http://www.cni.org/docs/ima.ip-workshop/Massarsky.html*.

Copyright Legislation

Further data on U.S. Copyright Law, and related laws contained in Title 17 of the United States Code, can be found online in Circular 92 at *http://www.copyright.gov/title17/92chap1.html*, which is provided by the U.S. Copyright Office. Further details on the U.K. Copyright legislation can be found online at *http://www.patent.gov.uk/copy.htm*.

10
Synchronization Rights and Royalties

**Definition ▪ Synch License ▪ Synch Fee ▪
Royalty Payment ▪ Master Use License**

Synchronization Royalties, or synch royalties, are license fees paid by media production and distribution companies to the copyright owner for a synchronization license that grants the right to use a song or melody in synchronization with visual images for public distribution and retail. Visual images would include motion pictures, commercials, television programs, and home videos.

Synchronization License
In the United States
In order to obtain a synchronization license in the U.S., the licensee must contact the music publisher directly, negotiate the conditions of use, and reach and sign a mutually binding agreement. When and how the licensee must pay the synchronization license fee is stipulated in the agreement.

Outside the United States
Mechanical rights societies in countries not including the U.S. frequently provide optional synchronization licensing services next to mechanical licensing services. When signing up for membership with an MRS, each prospective member must decide whether or not to grant the MRS the right to administer synch licenses. A MRS may provide three options to choose from: The synch licenses are either exclusively included, included on first call, or excluded from the control of the MRS.

Exclusively included means that the MRS has the exclusive right to negotiate and issue a license for the relevant use on behalf of the member. Included on first call means that the MRS has the right to negotiate and issue a license, though must get prior approval for the use from the member. Excluded means that the MRS has no right to negotiate or issue a license on the member's behalf.

A MRS may equally allow its members to select specific individual licenses, whether they be television programs, commercials, or motion pictures to be included or excluded from their control.

The U.S.-based MRS, The Harry Fox Agency, discontinued its synchronization licensing services in June 2002. Licensees will therefore have to contact the publisher directly. And how do they know which publisher to contact? They can search for U.S. publishers in the information databases made available by the performance rights organizations (ASCAP, BMI). Check their Web sites for further details.

Synchronization License Fee
Synch fees vary depending on the type of use, scope of the license, length of use, territory of exploitation, nature of the visual images, production budget, if the song will be released on a soundtrack album or other type of record, and the importance of the song in context with the visual images. Some types of use could be a visual performance or background use, while scope of the license includes broadcast rights for motion pictures, pay-per-view television, or home videos. The fee changes with each intended use.

Motion Picture Synchronization Royalties
Motion picture synch fees are determined by the placement and usage of a song in the film alongside its budget and cast. A song placed over the opening credits of a high-budget film starring several big-shot actors and a renowned director will run in the higher end range; a song or melody placed on the closing credits of an independent film will call for a lower synch fee. Whether or not a song is performed by one of the actors in a film or is used as theme or background music also has a bearing on the scale of the fee. The scope of synch license fees for motion picture licenses is vast, though on average runs between $15,000 and $50,000.

Commercial Synchronization Royalties
Commercials can turn out to be very lucrative for songwriters. It was reported, though not officially confirmed, that Microsoft paid the Rolling Stones between $8 and $14 million for the use of the song "Start Me Up" in their 1995 advertising campaign when launching their new operating system. Typically, though, a sum between $50,000 and $500,000 for a one-year usage limited to one nation is a more likely sum to be negotiated.

Payment Methods

Synch license fees can be paid out to the copyright owner in a number of ways:

- As a "one-time buy-out" fee where the licensee pays a one-time fixed sum to the licensor in return for all rights assigned to the licensee in perpetuity and without restrictions
- As a "limited buy-out fee" where the licensee pays a one-time sum to the licensor for a limited amount of sound carriers (DVDs, Videos, etc.) that can be sold without having to pay further royalties; when the limit is surpassed, further license payments are due
- On a "per-carrier sold" basis frequently used for home video tapes or DVDs
- On a "per-episode basis" frequently used for television theme songs
- For a limited duration in time, which is typically one, three or five years, a practice frequently used for commercials

The method of payment is dependent on the outcome of negotiations between the parties involved.

Master Use License

If a commercially released sound recording is to be used by the licensee, he will also need to get permission from the owner of copyright in the sound recording, usually the record label, by obtaining a "master use license." The master use license fees and conditions of use will also have to be negotiated by the parties involved.

For further details on the synch fees that are paid out, start off by checking the Web sites of the MRSs and PROs. Also check other books or the Internet. Professional advice from industry players is the best source of information.

11
Print Rights and Royalties

Definition ▪ Licenses ▪ License Fees ▪ Royalty Split

Print royalties are license fees paid by a music print publisher to the copyright owner for the right to sell and distribute copyrighted works in form of sheet music and folios to the public. Sheet music consists of printed music of a single song while folios contain a collection of songs. Ballads and guitar tab books are common examples of printed music.

Licenses
Licenses for print music are generally granted to the licensee for a limited term, usually three to five years, with an option of renewal. The licensor should pay attention to inventory management and sell-off rights of printed music when signing an agreement with the licensee.

License Fees
License fees are paid on a per-unit sold basis: For every single-song sheet of music sold, the licensor may receive 20% of the retail price; for every folio sold, the licensor may receive 10%–13% of the retail price. Fees vary and solely depend on what both parties, the licensee and licensor, have negotiated and agreed on in their contract. For folios containing selected copyrighted works by different songwriters, the pro-ration method is used to compute the royalties per contributor. This method is equally used for computing license fees in compilations. It is explained in detail in Chapter Nineteen under "Pro-rata Computed Results."

Royalty Split
Royalty split is what the author gets if he markets his printed music indirectly through a publisher: For single-song sheet music the author may only get $0.05–$0.10 U.S. cents per copy; for folios the author may receive about 10% of the wholesale price. However, publishing contracts are changing, and a 50/50 split between author and publisher of all earnings is already viable, resulting in higher print income for songwriters.

12
Additional Publishing Income

**DART Monies ▪ Blank Tape Levies ▪ Rental and Lending ▪
Translation/Adaptation ▪ Black Box**

We will now look at several other sources of secondary publishing income.

DART Monies
In the United States
The Audio Home Recording Act (AHRA) of 1992 requires[6] manufacturers and importers to pay royalty tax on digital audio recording devices and technology (DART) that are distributed in the United States. Examples are blank audio tapes, discs, or digital audio recorders. Blank CDs and CD burners used with computers are, in contrast, not subject to a DART royalty as they are "not manufactured for the purpose" of duplicating audio. This royalty is collected to compensate copyright owners and performers of music for the loss of revenues due to home recording. Information on DART can be found online at *http://www.copyright.gov/carp/dartfact.html*.

The royalties payable come in form of a tax: The AHRA imposes a tax on blank audio tapes of 3% of the wholesale price and a tax on digital audio recorders of 2% of the wholesale price. These royalties are deposited with the Copyright Office for further distribution among interested copyright parties, provided the copyright owners file a claim with the office during January and February of each year. A claimant can be anyone whose musical work or sound recording has been: (1) embodied in a digital or analog musical recording lawfully made and distributed; and (2) distributed in the form of digital or analog musical recordings or disseminated to the public in transmissions during the appropriate royalty payment period.

Royalties are allocated to claimants based on broadcast performances, or the number of airplays, and record sales during a set time period on a per-country basis. The numbers of each work a claimant has participated in is compared to the total number of all works during the same period.

The royalties collected and distributed are split two-thirds (66.67%) to one-third (33.33%) between:

- the copyright owner of the sound recording (SR—usually the record label), the featured artists, the non-featured artists (AFM), and the non-featured vocalists (AFTRA) who performed on the SR
- the publishers and authors of the corresponding musical and literary work

The exact breakdown awards the SR copyright owner 37.60%, featured artists 25.07%, AFM 2.80%, and AFTRA 1.20% of the 66% royalty split. Publishers and authors divide their 33% royalty split 50/50, so each party receives 16.66%.

The Alliance of Artists and Recording Companies (AARC) is the main U.S. organization representing featured artists and recording companies, both domestically and abroad, in the areas of home taping/private copy royalties and rental royalties. Detailed information can be found on their Web site at *http://www.aarcroyalties.net.* The agency represents publishers in the same area. Performing rights societies (PROs) handle DART monies on behalf of affiliated songwriters, provided that the latter have designated the PRS to do so when signing up for membership. Songwriters should enquire how DART monies are handled and check conditions and possible charges with the PROs before signing up.

Cross-border bilateral agreements exist between collecting societies. To give an example, the U.S.-based AARC currently collaborates with the following societies:

Territory	Society	Web site Address
Japan	CPRA	http://www.cpra.jp/web/e/index.html
Japan	RIAJ (Indy Labels)	http://www.riaj.or.jp/e/index.html
Spain	AIE	http://www.aie.es
Netherlands	SENA	http://www.sena.nl
Ireland	RAAP	http://www.raap.ie/

As we already learned in previous chapters, the MRSs and PROs equally collaborate through a network based on reciprocal agreements.

Blank Tape Levies
Outside the United States

Blank tape levies—also called blank media levies, blank media tax, private copying levy, or home taping tax—are collected from manufacturers and importers in other countries alongside the U.S.: Austria, Belgium, Bulgaria, Cameroon, Czech Republic, Denmark, Ecuador, Estonia, Finland, France, Gabon, Germany, Hungary, Iceland, Italy, Japan, the Netherlands, Nigeria, Poland, Romania, Slovenia, Spain, Switzerland, Ukraine, and Uzbekistan and others. Canada[7] equally has a blank media levy since 1997 when "Part VIII, Private Copying" was added to the Canadian Copyright Act. Finland has one of the highest blank media levies worldwide. The United Kingdom, Ireland, and Luxemburg, in contrast, are examples of countries that do not have a private copying levy.

Definitions on what recording devices and media the levies apply to and who the beneficiaries are differ from country to country. As opposed to the U.S., a levy is applied to blank CDs (CD-Rs) and CD burners in a number of countries listed above. For details on each of the national organizations that monitor, collect, and distribute blank media levies, check with your royalty collecting society, which is the MRS, PRO, or SR Performance Rights Societies (SRPROs). They will be able to point you to the right organization that will assist you in getting your questions resolved.

RCSs frequently have internal divisions that specifically focus on this task. The German society GEMA, for instance, has a division called ZPÜ (Zentralstelle für private Überspielungsrechte) that does just that. German levies to be paid by manufacturers, importers and distributors are listed online at *http://www.gema.de/musiknutzer/leerm edien_geraete/leermedien.shtml.*

Rental and Lending

Rental of DVDs/video films and audio carriers by videothèques, as well as lending of audio carriers or sheet music by libraries, is another source of income. Record rental royalties can bring considerable revenue in countries where record prices are high or where people are accustomed to renting audiovisual products that are available in public libraries.

In the United States

According to the Record Rental Act of 1984[8], no commercial rental, lease, or lending by owners who acquired copies of sound recordings

(SR) on or after October 4, 1984, is permitted without the authorization of both the copyright owners of the SR and the underlying musical works. When the authorization is granted to the owner, part of the revenues from rental and lending must be allocated to both copyright owners. Royalties between the copyright owners are split in the same way as are royalties of record sales.

AARC administers domestic and foreign rental royalties for its artist members. Artists who performed on U.S. recordings, as well as copyright owners of each SR and underlying musical work, are entitled to royalties from the rental and lending of their works in domestic and foreign territories. This is equally the case for foreign artists in other countries. Artists should check to ensure they have not granted their rights to record labels that would forfeit additional royalties from such rentals.

Outside the United States
Numerous countries next to the U.S. have laws similar to the Record Rental Act. The European Union (EU) implemented the Rental and Lending Directive in 1992[9]. Several amendments to the directive have been applied in subsequent years. Under the terms of Directive 92/100/EEC (Articles 1 and 5), authors and other rights holders have an exclusive lending right and the power to authorize or prohibit public lending of their works or other subject matter. According to Article 5 of the directive, each EU member state is required to establish a system to remunerate at least the authors of a work for income made though rental and lending. As was reported by the European Commission (EC)[10], certain EU member states have so far not fully implemented the 1992 directive. This has led the EC to pursue infringement cases against these member states.

Efforts are continuously being made by the EC to establish the same directive in all member states that benefit the rights holders, including countries that have recently joined or will join the EU in the next couple of years. CECUP was one of the projects that was launched in 1998 and was financed by the EC. It is currently run by the European Bureau of Library, Information and Documentation Associations (EBLIDA). CECUP's objective was to bring copyright awareness to the library community in ten central and eastern European countries—Bulgaria, the Czech Republic, Estonia, Hungary, Latvia, Lithuania, Poland, Romania, Slovakia and Slovenia—that have joined or will join the European Union in the future. You will find a complete list of EU member states online by visiting the Web site *http://europa.eu/abc/governments/index_en.htm.*

Other countries equally have rental and lending directives. Many follow the standards formulated in the TRIPS Agreement set forth by the TRIPS Council, all members being part of WTO (World Trade Organization). It came into effect on January 1, 1995, and is to date the most comprehensive multilateral agreement on intellectual property. WTO/TRIPS is part of a large network of international copyright and international trade treaties that focus on copyright protection. For more on TRIPS, visit the WTO Web site at *http://www.wto.org/english/tratop_e/trips_e/t_agm3_e.htm.*

Why is all this information necessary? Because as a rights holder and in particular as an author who hasn't granted his rights to another party, you are entitled to a share of the domestic and foreign income from the rental and lending of your works. Contacting the RSC you are affiliated with is the best place to start in order to find out further details of what you are entitled to.

Translation/Adaptation
Popular songs also find their way into foreign territories by translating the song lyrics and releasing and distributing cover versions that are frequently performed by well-known national performing artists in their local tongue. Works can moreover be adapted. This means that the existing lyrics of an original composition are modified or that new lyrics are added to pre-existing instrumental works. Lyric translation and adaptation are categorized as derivative works.

The publishers of the original works are entitled to publishing royalties from the exploitation of derivative works, as is the local lyricist. The latter regularly receives one-sixth of the combined total revenues from mechanical and performing royalties of both the writer's and publisher's share. This, however, depends on national regulations and on negotiation between parties. Should the arrangement of a work remain unchanged, and thus not be considered as a "new" derivative work, the remainder of income will be allocated to the original author and publisher. Should the arrangement be considered sufficiently original to be copyrightable, it will also be categorized as a derivative work. This rarely happens. The copyright owner will then equally receive his share of revenues. A commission may be deducted by a sub-publisher prior to distributing the revenues to the receiving parties if he is involved in securing the publishing deal.

A user who intends to release and distribute a derivative work must first obtain approval from the publisher of the original work. Both parties may be represented by their affiliated societies. Next to clarifying the royalty split, details regarding the term of agreement, copyright details to be published, publishing rights to be granted, and registration details with collecting societies are some of the particulars to be discussed. Registration details include the song titles and identification of cover versions in foreign territories to secure that money is correctly allocated to original copyright holders.

Black Box
The black box includes royalties collected by collecting societies from songs that are not registered or claimed by any publisher. In certain countries, unclaimed song revenues are periodically distributed to national publishers. Collaborating songwriters may equally participate in this source of income. Check with your collecting society for further details.

13
Digital Licensing

Definition ▪ Licensing ▪ Societies

Digital Music Services
Every Internet broadcast of a musical work

a) constitutes a public performance of that musical work
b) constitutes a public performance of the sound recording of that musical work
c) involves the reproduction and distribution of that musical work
d) involves the reproduction and distribution of the sound recording of that musical work;

To be authorized to offer a published, non-dramatic musical work that is not in the public domain for download or streaming on a Web site, or broadcast it via the Internet or via other digital means, the licensee must first obtain licenses from the different parties involved. The licensee will have to

a) contact the performing rights society that carries the song in its repertoire for a license to publicly perform the musical work
b) contact the mechanical rights society that carries the song in its repertoire or copyright holder, should he not be affiliated with a mechanical rights society, for a license to reproduce and distribute the musical work
c) contact the copyright owner in the sound recording, usually a record label or the author, for a license to reproduce, distribute, and publicly perform the sound recording of that musical work

Digital Licensing of published musical works is thus provided by mechanical rights societies, as well as by performing rights societies and copyright owners in the sound recordings. As we have seen in earlier chapters, income collected and distributed by mechanical and performance rights societies are publishing royalties paid out to authors and publishers, not to performing artists or record labels. We shall now explore which and how collecting societies handle digital licensing in the United States and the United Kingdom in more detail. We shall also look at the license types in details. Web links to relevant pages online are also included. I have included this section as part of this guide since digital licensing is a fairly novel area and the administration and services may not yet be clear to the readers.

Digital Licensing by Mechanical Rights Societies
In the United States
The mechanical rights society, The Harry Fox Agency (HFA), offers licensing under Section 115 of the U.S. Copyright Act for reproduction and distribution of musical works for various digital formats. The digital licenses currently administered by HFA are:

- Digital full-length audio-only permanent downloads (DPD)
- Limited use digital downloads
- Music subscription services
- On-demand streaming services
- New media downloads
- Phonic ringtones or pre-recorded ringtones

The first four license formats listed are broadly referred to as Internet licenses. Each digital license format is administered independently, and separate licenses are required by the licensee for the use and exploitation of a musical work. Ringtone, DPD (Digital Phonograph Delivery) and CD licenses, which are all administered by HFA, thus require three distinct authorizations.

Ringtones - The use of fragments or entire musical works as phone ringing tones involves both performing and mechanical rights. In many territories the local mechanical rights society can grant the necessary authorization for ringing tones. There is no Standard Contract for ringing tones.

Blanket licenses are commonly issued, whereas individual "per program" licenses are rarely issued, to licensees by colleting societies when dealing with Internet licensing. This is common practice and is applied by other mechanical and performing rights societies in the U.S. and abroad.

HFA may, however, not be authorized by a publisher to license a song for all license formats. This is dependent on the individual agreement between both parties. The music service provider, as the licensee, will have to contact the publisher directly should this be the case.

An online licensing facility is equally offered by HFA through a service called "Songfile" which enables users to directly license up to 2500 DPDs via the Internet. It is accessible on the HFA Web site at *http://www.harryfox.com/public/songfile.jsp*. Songfile also provides an online catalogue of all songs contained in the HFA repertoire including a per-song listing of the copyright related information available to the public. Licensees with established HFA Online accounts can also obtain DPD licenses using eMechanical. Digital licensing services provided by HFA are explained on their Web page at *http://www.harryfox.com/public/infoFAQDigitalLicensing.jsp*. The HFA Web site also provides a page that focuses on definitions of digital music terms including streaming, downloads, ringtones, SACD, Web casting and others. You can also contact the Harry Fox Agency via email by sending a request to *newmedia@harryfox.com*.

HFA handles U.S. licensing and thus only licenses digital music services that have their central servers located within the United States, including its territories and possessions and the Commonwealth of Puerto Rico. It does represent and collect for affiliated foreign MRSs as well. Details regarding rates and terms for statutory licenses for eligible non-subscription services to perform sound recordings publicly can be found at *http://www.copyright.gov/carp/webcasting_rates.html*.

In the United Kingdom
MCPS/PRS
The mechanical rights society MCPS offers licensing for reproduction and distribution of musical works for various digital formats in the U.K. Digital licenses for online music and mobile phone services currently administered by MCPS are divided into the following categories:

- Mobile phone ringtones
- Music on Web sites, including downloads and streaming
- Music for telephone on-hold services
- Premium Rate Telephone Services
- Podcasting

As is the case with HFA, each digital license format requires a separate authorization by MCPS. MCPS offers two approaches to clearing music online: "blanket licenses" and "prior approval." The publisher must opt for one of these two approaches. By selecting option two, clearances handled by MCPS are subject to the member's approval at all times.

The Joint Online License (JOL) and Limited Online Exploitation License (LOEL) are blanket license schemes that enable online music providers to clear the mechanical and performing rights administered by MCPS and PRS in a one-stop procedure. This is possible because MCPS and PRS work as an alliance and offer joint licensing schemes for the performance and broadcasting of music to the public. A licensee can also obtain licenses from MCPS and PRS independently.

To obtain a license from MCPS, go online and access the MCPS Web site at *http://www.mcps-prs-alliance.co.uk*. Relevant information is summarized in a section named "Music Users," or "Licensees". As part of the process, the licensee will have to first complete and submit the Online Clearance Request Form. Instructions on what to do and what to submit are provided online.

Other online licensing facilities are available for both MCPS and PRS members, licensees, and record labels who have signed up for membership to the Alliance Online Services. Membership is available to all online music providers. The Online Enquiry function also enables users to search for writer, publisher, product, and tune code information included in the repertoire. MCPS and PRS members have access to additional online facilities. Go online and check for details at *http://www.mcps-prs-alliance.co.uk/allianceonline*.

MCPS and PRS have set a joint royalty rate of 12% of total revenues for the online exploitation (JOL) of musical works. This rate is currently discounted to 8% of total revenues, though this may change in the future. LOEL license fees are equally published on the MCPS Web site.

MCPS handles U.K. licensing and only licenses digital music services that have their central servers located within the United Kingdom, including its territories, though also represents and collects for affiliated foreign mechanical rights societies. MCPS and PRS can be contacted by email by sending a request to onlinelicensing@mcps-prs-alliance.co.uk or by calling (++44) 020 7306 4991.

Digital Licensing by Performing Rights Societies
In the United States

The performing rights societies ASCAP, BMI, and SESAC all offer licensing for the public performance of a musical work for various digital formats.

BMI

The digital license formats currently administered by BMI are classified as New Media by market. The types of use are:

- Web sites
- Ringtones
- Mobile Entertainment
- Podcasting
- BMI Licensed Web sites

Information regarding the digital licensing options and agreements can be found online at *http://www.bmi.com/newmedia*. BMI offers two Internet related license fee schemes[11]: (1) the standard Web Site Music Performance Agreement; and (2) the Corporate Image License. The standard Web site license is generally for commercial entities that generate revenues from the operation of the Web site. It offers two financial calculations to determine the license fee based on the nature of a Web site. The "Gross Revenue" calculation is applicable if the licensee is using music as a primary feature on his Web site. The "Music Area" calculation allows the licensee to reduce the revenues subject to fee by factoring the traffic to pages with music in relation to his total Web site traffic. If the Web site's primary function is to promote an off-line business or generates little or no directly attributable revenue, the Corporate Image License is an alternative solution.

Further details relating to Web site licenses are summarized on the BMI Web site in the section labeled "Web Site FAQ" at *http://www.bmi.com/licensing/webcaster/webfaq.asp*. The term of the agreement, minimum fees payable, how to calculate license fees, and if 30-second song clips are exempt from licensing are some of the topics that are also covered. Reading through the Web-FAQ section helps songwriters to better understand how money is earned through digital licensing. Facts relating to other license types, including ringtones and podcasting licenses, can also be found online. The Digital Licensing Center (Klik-Thru) is an end to end automated online licensing system made available to licensees. Automated music usage reporting, digital fee payment systems, and other features are equally available online. Licensees can register online.

The commission rate deducted by BMI is currently quoted at around 15% of total revenues, with BMI members receiving the remainder. General questions can be forwarded to *weblicensing@bmi.com*.

ASCAP

The digital license formats currently administered by ASCAP are classified under New Media/Internet as:

- Non-Interactive for non-interactive sites and services
- Interactive for interactive sites and services
- Wireless Music (Ringtones and Ringbacks)

Information regarding the digital licensing options and agreements can be found online at *http://www.ascap.com/weblicense*. ASCAP offers three license fee schemes (called Rate Schedules) linked to Web sites: A, B, and C. Details can be found on the ASCAP Web page at *http://www.ascap.com/weblicense/feecalculation.html*. RateCalc® is an online tool equally provided by ASCAP to calculate estimates of license fees using each of the three rate schedules available. Go to *http://www.ascap.com/weblicense/license.html* for details. Further details relating to Web site licensing is summarized on the ASCAP Web site in the section labeled "Internet Licensing FAQs" at *http://www.ascap.com/weblicense/webfaq.html*. A "General Licensing Interactive System" provided to licensees is available, as is an online registration service tool for ASCAP affiliates.

The commission rate deducted by ASCAP is quoted at less than 12% of total revenues. General questions can be forwarded to *webLicense@ascap.com*.

SESAC

The digital license currently administered by SESAC is the
- On Line SESAC Internet Performance License

It grants authorization to publicly perform SESAC affiliated music on individual Web sites. This license covers such uses as live or archived performances, on-demand streaming, music videos, and song previews. Information regarding the SESAC Internet license agreement and related fees are available online at *http://www.sesac.com/licensing/internetLicensing.asp.* The Internet Agreement can be downloaded from the SESAC Web site. License fees are summarized on page 6 of the present agreement under Schedule "A." License requests can be submitted to SESAC online. An end-to-end automated online licensing system is currently not offered to licensees. Questions regarding additional new media license types can be forwarded to *internetlicensing@sesac.com.*

In the United Kingdom
MCPS and PRS work as an alliance. We covered details on digital licenses for the public performance of musical works earlier in this chapter

Digital Licensing in other countries
For digital licensing in other countries, please refer to the Royalty Collecting Society Directory in the back of this guide. Mechanical and performing rights societies are listed by country with Web links to online information. Several societies have comparable data as is presented in the preceding pages summarized on their Web sites. Or give them a call.

Copyright Legislation
U.S. Copyright legislations that address digital media are the Audio Home Recording Act of 1992, the Digital Performance Right in Sound Recordings Act (DPRSR) of 1995, and the Digital Millennium Copyright Act (DMCA) of 1998. In the U.K. the Copyright, Designs and Patents Act 1988 addresses digital media legislation.

14
Public Performance of Sound Recordings

Definition ▪ Master ▪ Licensing ▪ Commission Rates ▪ Societies ▪ Membership ▪ Royalty Split

In Chapters Seven through Twelve we looked at publishing income, which are monies primarily distributed to publishing companies and authors. But what license fees are paid out to performing artists and record labels? Public performance royalties for sound recordings, or masters, are monies paid out to performing artists when a sound recording is broadcast or played in public. As we shall see in this chapter, the regulations on what public performance license fees are compulsory differ by country. Artist royalties are also covered in Chapter Sixteen.

Public performance royalties for masters are thus license fees paid by the licensee to the copyright owner in the sound recording (SR) *and* to the performing artists for a performance license that grants the licensee the right to play, perform or broadcast the SR publicly.

Master
A master recording is the original sound recording of a musical and literary work that is produced in a recording studio from which subsequent copies are made that are distributed and sold. A master is, in contrast, not distributed to the public. Each individual composition has a corresponding master. An album comprising of twelve individual songs thus contains copies of twelve individual masters.

Copyright Owner in the Sound Recording
The copyright owner in the sound recording (SRCO) is usually the entity or person who financed the production and recording process. This is typically a record label, but can also be the artist.

Licensees
Licensees are broadcasters for radio and television stations—either terrestrial, satellite, or digital and analog cable—and Internet radio

stations that use SR in their transmissions. Other applicable arenas where you'd find broadcasters include clubs, shops, bars, pubs, restaurants, grills and other public venues, jukebox owners, and music users who play sound recordings in public.

Performing Artists
Performing artists are all featured artists, session/studio musicians, orchestral players, or singers/vocalists who performed on a sound recording that is broadcast on the radio or played in public.

Transfer of Rights
The member will exclusively transfer the public performance rights and broadcast performance rights in respect to the sound recordings to the SRPRO. Simulcasting rights, interactive and non-interactive Web casting rights, fully on-demand rights, or other new media rights may be transferred on a voluntary basis. Simulcasting rights are rights that allow simultaneous unaltered transmission of SR via the Internet next to free radio broadcasts. Non-compulsory rights that can be assigned by choice vary by society and by contract. Members who sign up should check the section "Assignment of Rights" in their agreement.

Sound Recording Performance Rights Societies
SR Performance Rights Societies (SRPROs), also referred to as broadcast royalties collecting societies, act as licensors and administer SR performance licenses and royalties on behalf of the affiliated SRCO record labels and performing artists in exchange for a percentage of the revenues collected from the exploitation of the SR.

Commission Rates
The commission rates vary between societies, though on average range from 10% to 20% of total revenues collected. 20% is on the upper side and includes the commissions that are additionally charged by foreign societies that collect overseas public performance, broadcast and associated income, should a SR be played or broadcast in public in countries abroad.

Royalty Split
The royalties paid out by the collecting societies are generally split between the beneficiaries. A 50/50 percent split computed on a track-by-track basis between the SRCO and the performing artists is not uncommon, though this varies from society to society. Performing artists may get paid directly by the society they are affiliated with or

indirectly via the SRCO. This depends on the policies and regulations set out by each society and whether or not a performing artist has signed up for membership with a society. As a rule, income can only be paid out by SRPRO to affiliated members directly.

Membership
SRCOs and performing artists can sign up for membership independently. A member can generally affiliate with one SRPRO per country only. Members do not forcibly have to be residents of that country to be eligible for membership. This depends on the rules set out by each SPPRS.

Membership Fees
There is generally no annual membership fee charged by a SRPRO.

Overseas Mandate
A member can decide to appoint one SRPRO as exclusive agent to negotiate, monitor, collect, and pay out overseas income on a worldwide or country by country basis by signing and submitting an overseas mandate. If and how this is possible depends on the policies outlined by each society. A SPPRS can only collect income in a foreign territory if a reciprocal arrangement is in place with the foreign SPPRS of that territory.

Registering and Tracking SR Performance Right Data
Some SRPROs offer online database tools that allow record labels to register and update, as well as performing artists to verify SR performance right data related to record releases, including details of the artist, song title, ISRC, catalogue number/bar code, full performer line-up, country of recording, and more.

Let's now look at the respective collecting societies in the United Kingdom and the United States.

Broadcast Collecting Societies
In the United Kingdom
PPL (Phonographic Performance Limited[12]) is a music industry organization that collects and distributes airplay and public performance royalties in the U.K. on behalf of over 3,500 record companies and 40,000 performers.

PPL - Overseas Income
PPL works co-operatively through reciprocal agreements with other

overseas record companies, currently nineteen, and performer societies, currently twelve, covering the largest music markets worldwide. PPL is equally the largest SPPRS worldwide. Further negotiations with other societies are ongoing.

PPL at present cooperates with the following record label societies:
Australia (PPCA) • Austria (LSG) • Belgium (SIMIM) • Brazil (ABRAMUS) • Canada (AVLA) • Denmark (GRAMEX (DK)) • Finland (GRAMEX (Fin)) • France (SCPP) • France (SPPF) • Germany (GVL) • India (PPL India) • Ireland (PPI) • Italy (SCF) • Japan (RIAJ) • Netherlands (SENA) • Norway (Gramo) • Serbia Montenegro (OFPYO) • Sweden (IFPI Sweden) • USA (SoundExchange)

PPL at present cooperates with the following performer societies:
Austria (LSG) • Belgium (URADEX) • Brazil (ABRAMUS) • Denmark (GRAMEX (Den)) • Finland (GRAMEX (Fin)) • Germany (GVL) • Ireland (RAAP) • Japan (CPRA) • Netherlands (SENA) • Sweden (SAMI) • Switzerland (SwissPerform) • USA (SoundExchange) •

Two other U.K. performer organizations, PAMRA and AURA, recently merged and their services and operations were fully integrated into PPL. PPL is thus responsible for collecting all U.K. performers' royalties.

Royalty Split
The PPL royalty income is split, according to the European Economic Community legislation known as the Rental Directive, 50/50 between record labels and performing artists on a track-by-track basis. This ensures that half of the total PPL revenue is paid out to performers, of which featured performers currently receive 65% and non-featured performers 35%. Producers cannot be members of PPL and thus cannot receive any money from the PPL, unless they apply as a record company. The producer's share is generally paid directly by the record label. PPL only pays members.

Payment
PPL only pays royalties directly to performing artists who are members. Alternatively PPL may pass on the collected royalties to the record label that, in turn, pays the performing artists according to the percentage stipulated in the record contract.

Registration
Performers need to register in order to obtain a PID (Performer Identification Number). This can be done either via the online Registration facility available at *http://www.royaltiesreunited.co.uk* or by calling U.K. Performer Services at +44 (0) 20 7534 1234. The PID will allow PPL to link performing artists and session musicians with

the recordings on which they have performed and to make distribution payments to them once they have submitted all the relevant information required.

Registering a Sound Recording
When registering a SR, PPL requires record labels to submit full recording details including notes on who has contributed with what performance to each recording by using an online computer database system called CatCo. The information stored can then be accessed by PPL, the MCPS, and other interested parties.

Chart Registration
Registering in the official U.K. and other national charts is also possible. More information can be found on the official charts Web site at *http://www.theofficialcharts.com*, which is provided by BPI (British Phonographic Industry—the British record industry's trade association) and ERA (Entertainment Retailers Association).

Contact Details
For further details on PPL including how to apply for membership, visit their Web site at *http://www.ppluk.com* or contact PPL by phone at +44 (0) 20 7534 1000.

VPL
Video Performance Limited (VPL) is comparable to PPL, though is a U.K. organization set up by the music industry in 1984 to specifically administer the broadcast, public performance, and dubbing rights in music videos. VPL represents the copyright owners of music videos and currently has over 800 members comprising mainly, but not exclusively, record companies. There are over 45,000 music videos currently registered with VPL. For more information, visit the Web site at *http://www.vpluk.com*.

Another organization that may be of interest to artists is the Musicians Union. You can access their Web site online by going to *http://www.musiciansunion.org.uk/html/index.php*.

In the United States
SoundExchange
SoundExchange[13] is the first organization formed in 2000 in the United States to collect compulsory performance royalties for sound recording copyright owners, featured and non-featured artists. SoundExchange is an independent, non-profit performance rights

organization that currently represents over 3,000 record labels and thousands of artists. SoundExchange was set up to collect revenues defined in the 1995 Digital Performance Right in Sound Recordings Act (DPRA). Before 1995, U.S. copyright law, in contrast to other countries, did *not* provide a performance right in sound recordings and no SR performance monies were therefore collected and distributed to the artists and labels. This has now changed.

Licensees

The DPRA and the Digital Millennium Copyright Act of 1998 (DMCA), however, at present only grant a performance right in sound recordings for specific, narrowly defined public performances. Licensees who are required to pay SR performance royalties in the U.S. are limited to:

- Digital cable and satellite television subscription services
- Non-interactive "Web casters"
- Satellite radio services (XM and SIRIUS)

This restriction does not apply to countries outside the U.S., such as Japan, Germany, France, Brazil, and the U.K.. SoundExchange does still *not* administer royalties for analog public performances (traditional FM radio and television) and on-demand services in the U.S. Radio stations can still perform copyrighted sound recordings free of charge. However, if stations simulcast their signal over the Internet or via satellite, performance royalties must be paid. SRs that are not "audio-only" (i.e., that are contained in films or on TV shows) are also license-free in the U.S. Licenses for interactive performances or reproduction of sound recordings through digital downloads must be obtained directly from the SCROs in the U.S.

Membership

No annual membership fee is required. As do other SRPROs, SoundExchange deducts a commission from the royalties collected. Details on how to sign up for membership are available online at *http://www.soundexchange.com/members/become_member.html.*

SoundExchange Overseas Income

SoundExchange works co-operatively through reciprocal agreements with other overseas societies. These are currently PPL (U.K.), SENA (Netherlands), and SOMEXFON (Mexico). Overseas SR performance royalties is a major source of income. U.S. performing artists should ascertain that they receive their share of royalties collected by societies in domestic *and* foreign territories. This may, however, also be dependent on the agreement between artist and record label as defined in the record contract signed by both parties. Artists should check for details on how SR performance royalties are handled with the record label. Limiting or excluding artists from this source of income is not acceptable.

SoundExchange also collaborates by distributing a share of gross revenues collected to members with the U.S. organizations AFM (American Federation of Musicians) and AFTRA (American Federation of Television and Radio Artists).

License Fees
Information regarding the present royalty rates payable by licensees can be found online at *http://www.soundexchange.com/rates.html* and at http://www.soundexchange.com/licensee_home.html.

Royalty Split
The SoundExchange royalty income is split on a track-by-track basis as follows: 50% SRCO, 45% featured artist, 2.5% AFM for non-featured musicians, and 2.5% AFTRA for non-featured vocalists.

Payment
SoundExchange collects and directly distributes royalties to members *and* non-members.

SoundExchange is currently the only organization designated to collect SR performance royalties. For further information, visit the Web site at *http://www.soundexchange.com.* Access the FAQ and the "About SoundExchange" section for more details. You can also contact SoundExchange by phone at 1-202-828-0120 or by email at *info@soundexchange.com.*

Other Broadcast Performance Rights Societies
For additional information on SRPROs in other countries, I have included a list with names and corresponding Web links below. Please note that the list is not exhaustive.

Territory	Society	Web site Address
Austria	LSG	http://www.lsg.at
Australia	PPCA	http://www.ppca.com.au
Belgium	SIMIM	http://www.simim.be

Territory	Society	Web site Address
Belgium	URADEX	http://www.uradex.be
Brazil	ABRAMUS	http://www.abramus.org.br
Canada	ACTRA	http://www.actra.ca
Canada	AVLA	http://www.avla.ca
Denmark	GRAMEX (DK)	http://www.gramex.dk
Finland	GRAMEX (FI)	http://www.gramex.fi
France	ADAMI	http://www.adami.fr
France	SCPP	http://www.scpp.fr
France	SPEDIDAM	http://www.spedidam.fr
France	SPPF	http://www.sppf.com
Germany	GVL	http://www.gvl.de
Ireland	PPI	http://www.ppiltd.com
Ireland	RAAP	http://www.raap.ie
Italy	IMAIE	http://www.imaie.it
Japan	CPRA	http://www.cpra.jp/web/e/index.html
Netherlands	SENA	http://www.sena.nl
Norway	GRAMO	http://www.gramo.no
Spain	AIE	http://www.aie.es
Sweden	SAMI	http://www.sami.se
Switzerland	SWISSPERFORM	http://www.swissperform.ch
United Kingdom	PPL	http://www.ppluk.com
USA	SOUNDEXCHANGE	http://www.soundexchange.com

15
Authorizations, Transfers, and Payments

I have chosen the U.K. as a showcase to display, by means of a flowchart, how each of the entities and players involved in the music industry collaborate with one another. These are explained in preceding and subsequent chapters.

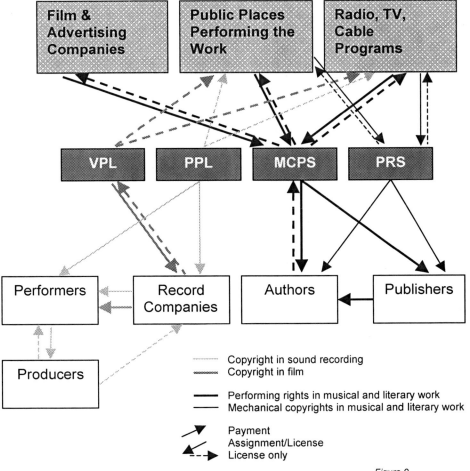

Figure 9.

16
Artist Royalties

**Definition ▪ Royalty Rate ▪ Negotiation ▪
Royalty Rate Computation ▪ Deductions ▪ Industry Numbers**

The artist royalty is the royalty payment based on the negotiated royalty rate agreed upon by the recording artist and the record label as defined in the record contract. This agreement holds the record company responsible to pay the recording artist for the exploitation of a sound recording. It is linked to the copyright in the sound recording (SR).

More accurately, the artist's royalty represents the artist's share of the proceeds made from the sale of his records, primarily in retail stores. Royalties are generally computed from the total number of records sold, not shipped or returned or exchanged, in stores. It is the chief source of income for a recording artist. Artist royalties earned through online sales is a source of income that is growing in importance.

Artist Royalty versus Mechanical Royalty
Reminder. The mechanical royalty and the artist royalty are two separate things. The mechanical royalty belongs to publishing royalties and is derived from the copyright in musical and literary works that is owned by and paid out to the publisher. The artist royalty is a separate source of income derived from the copyright in the sound recording that is owned by or licensed to the record label and paid out to the recording artist. Both royalties are, however, paid by one and the same entity—the record company.

Copyright in a Sound Recording
The copyright of a particular sound recording, or master, is owned by the record label *or* by the recording artist whereby:

- The record label either owns the legal rights to the sound recording, usually when the production and mastering process have been financed by the record label, which is common practice

- The sound recording is licensed by the recording artist (licensor) to the record label (licensee) for a specified term, which is often the case for experienced artists with a track record

Record
A record includes any medium or device containing audio recordings such as CDs, MDs, or cassette tapes. It may also include audiovisual recordings, such as DVDs, Videos, and other new media formats. The exact definition can be found in your record contract.

Royalty Rate
The royalty rate, stated in a percentage, is used to compute the artist's royalty, stated in dollars and cents, for each record sold and before deductions are considered. The current industry norm of recording artist royalty rates ranges from 10 to 22% of SRLP in the U.S., and from 14 to 20% of PPD in the U.K. and other parts of Europe.

Royalty Rate Negotiations
The recording artist's royalty rate is negotiated between the royalty paying company—usually the record label—and the artist being signed to the company. This contrasts the mechanical royalty rate which is, with the exception of the U.S. and Canada, dictated by copyright law and not negotiable. The royalty rate varies and depends on the artist's bargaining power. Is he a newcomer, a midlevel, or an established artist with a track record? Can he demonstrate a high level of studio and live experience? Does he have a fan base locally, statewide or nationally? Is the quality and marketability of the material to be released convincing? The more the artist has to offer the more he can bargain for. Keep in mind that a higher royalty is not necessarily the one and only thing the artist should focus on when he starts negotiating.

Method of Royalty Calculation
In the U.S. and Canada the artist's royalty is based on a percentage of the record's suggested retail list price or as a percentage of the record's wholesale price. Outside the U.S. and Canada the royalty is generally based on the published price to dealer (PPD), which is equal to the record's wholesale price. Let's look at both practices:

SRLP
The suggested retail list price (SRLP), also referred to as the

suggested list price, is generally the record's sticker price. This is the non-discounted, top line, full retail price for a new record release at a record store. It does not correspond to the average retail price paid by customers in record stores; this is because prices vary from store to store. SRLP is not a fixed number and changes according to the place and region it is sold. It commonly ranges from $14.98 to $17.98.

Wholesale Price
The wholesale price corresponds to the amount the record label charges the retailer for a record. It is by and large equivalent to less than half the SRLP because retailers pay significantly less for the record than what they sell it for. The royalty based on the wholesale price is therefore slightly more than twice the royalty based on SRLP. As a rule: the lower the SRLP or wholesale price, the lower the starting point of your royalty calculation.

The first two things the artist should thus look at in your contract are:

- Royalty rate
- Method of royalty computation used (SRLP or wholesale)

This is the *starting point* of the royalty calculation. The full royalty rate without deductions is also referred to as the headline rate or top line rate. There are other criteria to consider in your calculation, which we will look at now.

Deductions
Royalty paying companies use a variety of techniques in order to reduce their royalty payment obligations. When negotiating the clauses in your recording contract, you should look at any type of deduction the record company may try to impose on you. They will try to fight through most of these points by using compellingly sounding arguments. You may concede on some and push through certain other points. However, to be able to do this, it is important for you to understand them. I have listed a number of contract negotiation points and deductions that you may encounter in your contract below.

In our explanation below, every deduction or point of negotiation is marked with a letter (i.e., A, B, C, etc.). The following abbreviations are used: N = Negotiate • A/N = Acceptable, but to be negotiated according to points listed thereafter • N (__%) = Negotiate down to the percentage stated in brackets • RO = Rip off (do not accept and negotiate; delete this clause from the contract).

Examples will be provided below for better understanding. We will use the SRLP as method of computation and the following numbers in our example:

```
SRLP for CD equals            $14.99
Artist Royalty rate is        10% of SRLP
Royalty before deductions     $1.49/per CD sold
```

A. Container Charge *(Packaging deduction)*
Covers the record's cost of packaging charged to the artist ▪ Stated as a percentage of SRLP ▪ Industry norm: 20% for cassette tapes; 20 or 25% for CDs, DVDs and new media records; rates may vary. ▪ **N** (5–10%): Push down the rate, as packaging costs are greatly overstated. Any packaging deduction linked to Internet sales (i.e., downloads or subscription) should be barred.

```
SRLP less Container Charge equals Royalty Base
The SRLP is $14.99 and 20% of 14.99 equals $2.99
$14.99 - 2.99 = $12.00
```

After deducting the container charge, you obtain the **royalty base** or **royalty base price**. In the U.S. it is common practice to apply the royalty rate against the royalty base and *not* against the SRLP.

```
Royalty Base times Royalty Rate
$12.00 x 10% = $1.20
Adjusted royalty: $1.20/per record sold
```

This practice may also be employed in the U.K., (that is, PPD minus packaging charge). In our example, the royalty would thus be $1.20. This is what you, as an artist, get for each record sold. At times, the royalty is even computed on the PPD minus discounts. However, there are further possible deductions you may encounter in your contract:

B. 90% of Net Sales
Covers the practice of deducting 10% from your royalty of records sold (i.e., you are paid 90% royalty of the records sold) ▪ An explanation as to why 10% is deducted is not always given. To cover the cost of breakage (i.e., breakable records) has been one explanation used in the past. The word "breakage" is no longer used in contracts nowadays. ▪ This deduction should be barred from the contract, except possibly when shipping vinyl records. ▪ **RO**

```
Using our example:
Present Royalty times 90%
$1.20 x 90% = 1.08
Adjusted royalty: 1.08/per record sold or $1080
for 1000 records sold
```

C. Free Goods

Covers the practice of deducting 10%–25% from the total number of records shipped and thereby reducing your overall royalty per record sold • Record companies may justify this deduction as part of a 1) "New release" merchandising campaign (i.e., records offered in bundles with T-shirts and posters), 2) Special sales plan (i.e., free records offered as an incentive to retailers to reduce the overall price they have to pay per record when buying them in bulk), or 3) Promotional campaign (i.e., free copies sent to radio stations) • These discounts may appear on several non-related places in your contract and may be labeled differently. Pay attention. They add up • Free goods are royalty free • Industry norm: 15% royalty-free rate (*or* 85% royalty-bearing rate) of records shipped • Record companies can alternatively omit the free goods deduction from your record contract by lowering the record's wholesale price. The deduction would, however, still be accounted for, though would not be clearly visible to you. • **N** (5–10%): 1) Push down the free goods rate to 5–10% and set a cap to this number. 2) "Records sold," also labeled as "Record Sales," should be defined as 100% of records shipped, sold, and not returned to the label. 3) Persist on having all records shipped and accounted for as free goods listed separately (i.e., as a percentage of records shipped).

```
Records shipped times Royalty-bearing rate
times Adjusted Royalty
100% - 15% = 85% (royalty-bearing rate)
1000 x 85% = 850 (number of royalty-bearing
records)
850 x 1,08 = $918
Adjusted royalty: $918 for 1000 records shipped
```

At 1000 records shipped and taking into account the 15% royalty free rate and 90% Net Sales deduction, you receive a royalty of $918, given that all records are sold and taking no other deductions into account. To state it differently, your royalty is reduced from $1.08 to $0.91 per record sold as a result of both deductions.

```
Present royalty times Royalty-bearing rate
1.08 x 85% = $0.91 (or 918/1000)
```

```
Adjusted royalty: $0.91/per record sold
```

D. Return Privilege
Covers a practice (limited primarily to the U.S. and Canada) that allows retailers in the music industry to ship back unsold records to the record company for a full 100% refund of their purchase price. In the U.K. this practice is also at times in use, allowing retailers to return up to 5% of records distributed to them. The practice is employed to minimize the retailer's risk. The artist does not receive any royalties for unsold and returned records. • **N** (20-30%): Try to set a limit to the number of unsold records the retailer can return (i.e., 20–30% of records shipped). This is difficult to push through.

E. Reserve *(Reserve against returns)*
Due to the 100% return privilege, the record company, on its part, delays payment of a portion of the artist's royalties linked to the records shipped to the retailers. As the record company cannot equally predict how many unsold records will be returned, this practice is employed to minimize risk and avoid overpaying the artist. The reserve is paid out after a set period of time • Industry norm: 35% of records shipped for a period of one year • **A/N**: 1) Accept 35%, though not more. As a newcomer, this may be difficult. 45% max. 2) Make sure the contract specifies 35% of records shipped and not 35% of records sold. 3) Limit the reserve period to six months. Due to digital technology, this is ample time to compute if records shipped have been sold. 4) Press for payment of interest on the amount due (as the money paid by the retailer will be credited to a bank account and amass interest.) 5) If the period should extend over several accounting periods, which usually last 3 or 6 months, ask to split the reserve into equal amounts to be paid out per period. • Do note that this practice is a delay of the royalty payment and hence not a real deduction. It does influence the amount of money you will have in your pocket, which for new-coming and mid-level artists is of great importance.

```
Royalty less Reserve
Present royalty = $918 (see A. - C. for details)
$918 x 35% = $321.30 and $1020 - 321.30 = $596.70
Adjusted royalty: $596.70
```

F. Recoupment of Advances
Covers the practice of a record company to deduct a portion or all of the artist's royalties earned for the reimbursement of advances.

These are funds, called recoupable advances, paid to the artist prior to the release of a record to help finance business-related and, in part, personal expenditures. ▪ Advances are only to be recovered through royalty related income made from the sale of records in record stores. Make sure this is clearly specified in your contract. They should not be paid back by the artist using other income sources, such as mechanical royalties or Internet sales ▪ Each advance is listed and defined in your contract. Examples of direct advances: Money covering personal living costs. Examples of indirect advances: Recording expenses, studio equipment, transportation, video production costs, tour support, union scale (minimum amount to be paid to union members) ▪ Certain costs should not be considered as recoupable or partially recoupable advances: Record manufacturing, distribution, promotion, advertising, and marketing. ▪ N: 1) Be sure the costs just listed are non-recoupable. 2) Master recording costs, usually the largest expense, are usually 100% recoupable. So be sure to put a cap on the recording and production budget ▪ Get the record label to pay for the video production expenses since it is a promotional tool or split expenses 50/50; thus 50% recoupable. Be sure to put a cap on the amount to be spent per video. 3) Try to get 50% recoupable on tour support. 4) Promotional expenses, including outsourcing to independent promoters, should be non-recoupable. 5) Television advertising: 0% or up to 50% non-recoupable, on an approval basis only. 6) Artwork: non-recoupable. 7) Management and legal costs: non-recoupable. 8) All other expenses should be on an approval basis verified in writing.

G. Controlled Composition Clause

The controlled composition clause covers the practice of the record company to push for, and the artist to accept, a reduced mechanical royalty rate for any song the artist performs as part of his repertoire of which he is also the author. This ordinarily applies to writers who perform their own songs (i.e., writer = artist). Note that the author of the work can also be the person to whom copyright in the musical and literary work has been granted and who therefore controls it. The controlled composition clause is mainly applied by record companies in the U.S. and Canada. ▪ A reduced mechanical royalty rate, also called a reduced statutory rate is defined in the controlled composition clause in a record contract. ▪ Deductions come in two forms: 1) Reduced statutory rate; usually 75% of the full statutory rate per song 2) which is payable for a limited number of songs per album; usually limited to ten songs per album ▪ Inserted in newcomer and mid-level act contracts; Big name artists can, in general, bar these clauses from their contracts and, at times, even demand a minimum aggregate mechanical rate per album; that is, they will receive the statutory rate for a fixed number of songs (twelve or fourteen) regardless of the actual amount of songs contained on the album that is released. This can turn out to be not a deduction of, but an addition to, royalties earned for the artists. • **N:** 1) Try to get the controlled composition clause barred from your contract. 2) If not, try to limit it to specific types of record releases, such as "Greatest Hits" or compilations. 3) Try to bar the limit on the number of songs that receive a royalty.

Reminder. The mechanical royalty is paid by the record company to the copyright owner. The controlled composition clause is an attempt to reduce the record company's total royalty costs (e.g., the artist's, producer's, and mechanical royalties).

Further Deductions
There are further deductions that are often found in record contracts. Several are listed below. They basically deal with the aspects of where, how, and when a record is sold. Let's look at them below:

- ***Foreign Territory Sales Deduction,*** also referred to as overseas territory sales deduction or reduction: The territories that apply may be specified one by one and/or may be labeled as "Rest of World" • Covers the practice of reducing the headline royalty rate by ⅓ (33.3%) and at times even by half for records not sold in the domestic market. • **N:** 1) Try to limit the contractual number of foreign territories where a reduction applies (i.e., western democratic countries with binding economic ties should not be included). 2) Limit the foreign sales reduction to a maximum of ⅓ (minus 33.3%) of the headline rate. 3) For all-in agreements, ensure that the producer accepts similar pro rata reductions.
- ***New Medium Deduction,*** also called new format, new technology, new media, or new configuration reduction: Covers the practice of reducing the royalty rate by as much as 25%—rates may vary by medium—for manufacturing and distributing records/sound recordings using new technology. It is employed by record companies to cover the higher per unit costs of production. CDs are at times still considered a new medium. • **RO:** Exclude CDs from the list of new medium deductions, should this have been built into the contract. **N:** 1) Negotiate what technology is to be included as new medium in

the contract. 2) Try to exclude Internet related media (mp3, wma, etc.) from the list, as this distribution channel actually leads to cost-savings for the record company compared to alternative distribution channels. 3) Stipulate each new format in the contract. 4) Negotiate reduced rates.

- ***Type of Sale Deduction***: Covers the practice of reducing the royalty rate by as much as 50% linked to the type of record sold or the price it is sold for. Examples of record types are compilations by one artist, such as "Best of" and "Greatest Hits," or compilations by multiple artists. Examples of price-based reduction are records sold at mid-level or budget-level retail prices. **·** **RO:** Compilations that are released by the record label the artist signed to should not suffer a rate reduction. **N:** 1) Compilations by third party labels or distributors may require a rate reduction, which should not exceed 33% of the normal rate. 2) Check the definition of mid-priced and budget records in your record contract. Be sure to set the ceiling rate of both levels as low as possible. They are defined as a percentage of SRLP. Percentages do vary. Example: A record may be defined as a budget record when it sells at 55% or less of SRLP; a record may be defined as a mid-priced record when it sells in excess of 55% and below 75%. 3) Negotiate reduced rate levels for each discount level: ⅔ (66.6%) of the royalty may be paid for mid-priced records, 50% for budget records.
- ***Mode of Sales Deduction***: Covers the practice of reducing the royalty rate by as much as 50% for records sold through specified retail channels. Examples are record clubs, covering more than 20% of album sales in the U.K., as well as phone order and mail order services. **N:** Negotiate reduced rate.

Contracts regularly contain phrases such as "but not limited to" or "including, without limitation," which broaden the playing field of the record labels. Be sure to bear this in mind when going over a contract.

The information provided in the preceding pages is intended to give artists who are in the midst of contractual negotiations with record labels some help in identifying important clauses and phrases that might be scattered throughout a record contract. As we have learned from this chapter, the top line royalty rate and the royalty is reduced in quite a number of ways, thus diminishing the overall income earned by the artist made per record sold. So pay attention prior to signing a record contract. We will look at contract terminology in the next chapter.

Industry Numbers

The SRLP for newly released album CDs by established artists in the U.S. ranges from $15.98 to $17.98, and for new released cassette tape albums from $9.98 to $11.98. Due to growing competition from new digital media services through online downloading and peer-to-peer file sharing services, as well as CD piracy, record sales via traditional sales channels have declined. To fight this negative trend, record labels and retailers have in part lowered wholesale and retail prices, effecting the SRLP. The SRLP may more likely be lowered and range from $13.98 to $15.98. You will continue to see new releases selling for $17.98 for superstar acts, though to a lesser extent.

It is a fact that record companies directly control the record's wholesale price and indirectly have an effect on the SRLP. How far record sales continue to be harmfully affected by digital media services remains to be seen. Looking at the RIAA 2005 Year-End Statistics[14], 705 million CDs were shipped *and sold* in 2005. In 2000, this number was 942 million, whereas in 1995 it was back down at 723 million. This shows that numbers have fluctuated even before digital media services came along. What causes this fluctuation is not the subject of this book. What is important for artists is to pay attention to markets and real numbers to confidently argue against all the "supposedly necessary" deductions brought in by record labels to undermine their negotiating position.

Information on the U.S. music industry's overall sales figures can be examined by accessing the Web site of the Recording Industry Association of America (RIAA) at *http://www.riaa.com*. RIAA is a trade group that represents the U.S. recording industry. The annual report published by each record company is another source of information, as are articles published in specialized trade magazines or Web sites that scrutinize the music industry's doings.

17
Contract Glossary

Defining Contract Terminology

In this chapter, I will explain terminology that is linked to record or publishing contracts. A contract is also called a deal or an agreement. A record contract may contain more than forty pages; publishing contracts are generally less voluminous. The sheer size of the contract, length of sentences, number and arrangement of clauses, headings, subsections, and the legal terminology used within may seem intimidating. You should therefore be factual in your approach. When looking at a contract, always ask yourself:

- Do I understand each term used in the contract? What is each term based on? How and where is it defined?
- Is there a cross-reference to other clauses in the contract?
- Do I understand the meaning of each sentence in the contract?
- What does each number mean; what is each number or percentage based on?
- Are there any ambiguities in the contract?

If any of these points are not clear to you, do not sign the contract. Read through the contract several times, ask friends or business partners, or seek legal device. And don't get pushed into signing a contract.

Contract Structure

The terms of a contract are usually arranged in clauses that are marked by headings and sub-headings. However, each term may appear several times throughout the contract and the definitions of the same term may differ from a previous definition provided. This is important to note. Do not assume that a definition you saw in one clause is necessarily identical to a definition in another clause. Certain terms may not be clearly visible to the reader at all. And don't expect the terms to be ordered chronologically or in alphabetical order. Many contract disputes involve disagreements that pertain to the interpretation of contract terms that are vague or ambiguous. Let's now look at further glossary terms you might encounter when discussing and negotiating your contract:

Advances
Pre-payment of direct and indirect monies by the record label or producer to the artist are called advances. Direct advances are living expenses paid out to the artist usually during the period prior to and shortly after releasing a record. Indirect advances are monies related to the production and promotion of a record, such as expenses relating to master recording, video production costs, and tour support. Some of the advances are recoupable, some are partially recoupable.

All-In royalty agreement
In an All-In royalty agreement, the artist would equally have to pay the producer's royalty out of his own royalty. The producer's royalty rate is typically between 2–4%. If the artist earns a 10% royalty and the producer's royalty rate is 2%, the artist would receive 8% of the SRLP.

Copyright Reversion
One talks of copyright reversion if the copyright of a work is reverted from the assignee, or publishing company, to the assignor, or copyright owner. It is generally found in a publishing agreement. Copyright reversion may occur if a song is not recorded or commercially released within a set term stipulated in the contract, typically measured from the moment the agreement has been signed.

Co-writer Deal
A co-writer deal is a collaboration with another writer. It is recommended that a song share agreement be set up and signed between the writers of a song. The royalty split related to the lyrical and musical contributions of both parties in a work should be stipulated therein. Examples: Both parties have contributed 50% each to both music and lyrics; or writer A has solely (100%) created the lyrics, writer B has (100%) composed the music. Or somewhere in between. This will avoid nasty disputes in the future.

Commercially Satisfactory
Delivering a commercially satisfactory record can include delivering technically acceptable master recordings, assuring sample clearances, and providing a list of session and performing artists who made contributions on the record. The exact definition will be stipulated in the contract. (See also delivery requirements.)

Creative Control

The party in charge of creative control has the final say on the artistic decisions linked to the production and promotion of a record. This may include the final selection of songs to be included on a record release, the producer and personnel involved in the production, mixing and mastering, the studios and equipment to be used during the production, artwork used for the record, location, producer, theme of video production, and control over the record production budget. Before signing an agreement, both the artist and record label should have a clear understanding of which party is in charge of creative control. Both parties can decide mutually or one of the two parties has the final say. This should be stipulated in the contract. Creative control may also entail (as part of European contracts) the moral rights that are owned by the author.

Cross-Collateralization

Also referred to as cross-recoupment. Should the artist agree to it, the record company can use royalties from one album to recoup advances from another album. Artists should try to bar this from the record agreement.

Delivery Requirements

Refers to the commitment made by the artist or band when signing the record contract to deliver a completed work to the record label according to a contractually set timetable (i.e., the delivery schedule and delivery date). Should the record be accepted as commercially satisfactory, it is considered delivered. Late delivery is frequently penalized by record labels, so checking and understanding the contract terms is critical and should be taken seriously by the artist signing the contract.

Escalation

Incentive for artists: Automatic, for every new album released or sales-based when reaching a set sales target (i.e., 250K, 500K, or 750K records sold) royalty rate increase; usually by 0.5%.

Grant

Refers to the assignment or licensing of specific rights to individual parties.

Master Recording Costs

Master recording costs may include all expenses related to the recording, production, mixing, and mastering of the master sound recording. Travel, living, and transportation expenses that are linked to the production of the master may also be incorporated.

Release Commitment

A release commitment is a firm pledge by the record company to release (i.e., deliver, distribute, put in stores for sale) a record at a contractually set date in a stipulated territory. Marketing and promotion commitments also exist.

Sample Clearance

Sample clearance deals with getting permission from the copyright owner to copy and reproduce a sample. Should you use a sample from a commercially released sound recording, you will need to contact both the copyright owner of the sound recording and of the musical and/or literary work. If you replay the sample yourself, you will only have to contact the latter. A short drumbeat or guitar sequence may already constitute a sample.

Term of Contract

(1) The term of a contract defines the amount of time the artist will be legally bound to cooperate with the record label. The term is usually divided into several periods: The initial period, the options periods, and the restriction period. Record labels may sign artists to a five or six-album deals (long-term commitment) or a one-album deal with one option (short-term commitment). Major record labels more often sign long-term; independent labels more often go for short-term deals. (2) The terms of a contract are obligations set forth in writing that each signing party is required to perform and which are enforced by law. Most of the terms are generally negotiable by the signing parties—the record label and the artist.

Territory

Refers to the geographic region covered by the contract.

18
More on Copyright

Copyright Registration ▪ **WIPO** ▪ **Copyright Protection** ▪
Duration of Copyright ▪ **Copyright Notice** ▪
Notice for Phonorecords of Sound Recordings

Copyright Registration
Official registration at a national copyright or patent office is not required to secure a copyright. It is, however, possible in a number of countries.

In the United States
It is important to note that the U.S. is the only country where you do need to register your work in order to claim your rights. In other words, copyright registration is required for works of U.S. origin before a copyright infringement lawsuit may be filed in U.S. Federal Court. A copyright infringement is a violation of copyright laws and occurs when your work is used without your authorization.

Copyright registration establishes a public record of the copyright claim. The copyright owner, regardless of his domicile or nationality, can register an original work with the Copyright Office in Washington, D.C. There are several application forms to choose from. To register an original published or unpublished work of the performing arts including musical and dramatic works, motion pictures and other audiovisual works, submit the copyright application Form PA. To register an original published and unpublished sound recording, submit the copyright application Form SR. And use the Form CA for supplementary registration to correct or amplify information given in the Copyright Office record of an earlier copyright registration.

For copyright purposes, there is a difference between musical compositions and sound recordings[15]: A musical composition consists of music, including any accompanying words, and is normally registered as a work of performing arts. The author of a musical composition is generally the composer and the lyricist, if any. A musical composition may be in the form of a notated copy, like sheet music, or in the form of a phonorecord, like a record. A sound recording results from the fixation of a series of musical, spoken, or other sounds. The author of a sound recording is the performer whose performance is fixed, or the record producer who processes the sounds and fixes them in the final recording, or both.

Copyright in a sound recording is not the same as, or a substitute for, copyright in the underlying musical composition. Although they are separate works, a musical composition and a sound recording may be registered together on a single application if ownership of the copyrights in both is exactly the same. To register a single claim in both works, complete Form SR. Give information about the author of both the musical composition and the sound recording.

By the way, you can register two or more unpublished songs, musical works in form of sound recordings, or song lyrics with one application and fee. This is done by registering these sound recordings under a single collection title. However, it is only possible under certain conditions stated in the Copyright Office regulations[16]. One of those conditions is that the copyright owner or owners must be the same for all the songs. Copyright belongs to the author and can be transferred only by a written agreement or other legal means. If there has been no transfer and the songs are by different authors, this copyright ownership requirement has not been met. An additional requirement is that there must always be at least one author common to all the songs, even if there has been a transfer of ownership. For further details, go online and download Circular 50 provided by the U.S. Copyright Office at *http://www.copyright.gov/circs/circ50.pdf*.

Where to register
To register a work, send the following three elements in the same envelope or package to:

The Library of Congress ▪ Copyright Office ▪ 101 Independence Avenue, S.E. ▪ Washington, D.C. 20559-6000 ▪ USA

1. A properly completed application form. Fill-in forms are available online. (See Web site link below.)
2. A non-refundable filing fee of $45 for each application. Checks, money orders, or bank drafts are accepted (no cash payments) and should be made out to: Register of Copyrights. (The fee was increased from $30 to $45 on July 1 2006.)

3. A non-returnable deposit of the work being registered. As the deposit requirements vary in particular situations, check the U.S. Copyright Office Web site for details.

At times, the owner of copyright is also referred to as "the publisher," although this may be confusing in case the copyright holder is the author himself. The author can, however, assign his copyrights in a work to a publisher, who then registers the work at the Copyright Office in the publisher's own name as owner of copyright. If the assignment of copyright is contractually signed by both parties, this is legitimate. A transfer of copyright for works already registered is also possible.

More information on U.S. copyright, copyright registration, and copyright transfer can be found on the informative Web site of the United States Copyright Office at *http://www.copyright.gov*, which is part of the U.S. Library of Congress in Washington D.C.

In the United Kingdom
In the U.K., there is no official register for copyright. It is an unregistered right, unlike patents, registered designs, or trademarks. There is no official action to take when a work is created in the U.K. Copyright registration is not a requirement in order to claim your rights.

WIPO
The World Intellectual Property Organization (WIPO) provides contact information of the copyright, trademark, and patent offices of each member country on their Web site at *http://www.wipo.int/members/en*. Internet, Email, phone, fax, and address details are supplied. The list encompasses 183 member countries. Contact the office of the country of interest for enquiries regarding copyright law, copyright registration, and online copyright research services.

Copyright Protection
There are several other ways to protect a copyright besides copyright registration. You can place your works with a lawyer or legal firm, preferably those specializing in music and entertainment law. They are most likely the ones to offer this type of service. Not all legal firms do. Either a one-time fee for each of the works you deposit or an annual fee for a package deposit containing numerous songs will be charged. A one-time fee of £25 (US$46) per work or an annual fee of 85£ (US$157) per package with a limited amount of deposits per year

could be used as an indicator. Fees do vary. Published and non-published works, as well as fragmentary and incomplete melodies, can be deposited. A retainer agreement including the standard terms and conditions will need to be signed when submitting the material. Make sure to read all documents before signing anything. A confirmation should be sent back to you by the lawyer or legal firm upon receipt of the material showing, among other things, the work titles, copyright holder of each song, and the date of receipt printed on official company stationery. Depositing the package with a lawyer or legal firm can have an additional weight in court procedures, should your copyright be infringed; this is helpful because lawyers are known to keep track of anything submitted to them.

An alternative possibility you have to support the evidence relating to your authorship of the work is to put a copy of the work—on paper, tape, or CD/DVD—in an envelope, sign across the seal of the envelope, and send it to yourself by registered mail. Upon delivery, keep the registered receipt and the unopened envelope in a safe place. Note the title of each work contained within on the envelope for future reference, as you may forget this over time. It is the date stamp coupled with the fact that the package is unopened that constitutes the crucial evidence. It does not, however, guarantee that the envelope has not been tampered with. This is sometimes referred to as the "poor man's copyright solution."

Duration of Copyright
In the United States
A work that is created on or after January 1, 1978, is automatically protected from the moment of its creation for a term enduring for the author's life plus an additional seventy years after the author's death. In the case of a joint work prepared by two or more persons, the term lasts for seventy years after the last surviving person's death. For a work created prior to January 1, 1978, check the U.S. Office of Copyright Web site for the applicable law. For an anonymous work, a pseudonymous work, or a work made for hire the copyright endures for a term of ninety-five years from the year of its first publication or a term of 120 years from the year of its creation, whichever expires first. Publication means the distribution of copies to the public. When the copyright expires, the work goes into the public domain and is free for use by anyone. Duration of copyright is synonymous to life of copyright.

In the United Kingdom and Europe
Identical to the U.S., the copyright for musical, literary, dramatic, filmed, and artistic works in the European Union (EU) lasts for the author's lifetime plus seventy years thereafter. This also relates to the copyright of songs. In contrast, the copyright for sound recordings, computer-generated works and performances, and communications to the public right including broadcasts on Web sites, TV, and cable programs are protected for only fifty years from the year of publication. Typographical arrangements are limited to twenty-five years from the date of publication.

The Copyright Notice
The copyright notice is used only on "visually perceptible copies." Examples are CD and DVD covers and inlays or printed music. The notice for visually perceptible copies should contain all of the following three elements[17]:

1. The symbol © (the letter C in a circle), or the word "Copyright," or the abbreviation "Copr."

2. The year of first publication of the work, or for unpublished works the year the work was first fixed in tangible form. In the case of compilations or derivative works incorporating previously published material, the year and date of first publication is sufficient

3. The name of the owner of copyright in the work, or an abbreviation by which the name can be recognized, or a generally known alternative designation of the owner (Example: © 2006 Jack the Songwriter)

Certain types of works, such as musical, literary, or dramatic works, can be fixed not in "copies" but by means of sound in an audio recording. Since audio recordings, such as audio tapes and phonograph disks, are "phonorecords" and not "copies," the "C in a circle" notice is not used to indicate protection of the underlying musical, dramatic, or literary work that is recorded. The ℗ is used for this purpose.

The Phonorecords of Sound Recording Notice
Sound recordings are defined in U.S. law as "works that result from the fixation of a series of musical, spoken, or other sounds, but not including the sounds accompanying a motion picture or other

audiovisual work." Common examples include recordings of music, drama, or lectures. A sound recording is not the same as a phonorecord. A phonorecord is the physical object in which works of authorship are embodied. The word "phonorecord" includes cassette tapes, CDs, DVDs, LPs, 45 r. p. m. disks, as well as other formats.

The notice for phonorecords embodying a sound recording should contain all the following three elements:

1. The letter P in a circle, "℗"

2. The year of first publication of the sound recording

3. The name of the owner of copyright in the sound recording, or an abbreviation by which the name can be recognized, or a generally known alternative designation of the owner. If the producer of the sound recording is named on the phonorecord label or container and if no other name appears in conjunction with the notice, the producer's name shall be considered a part of the notice (Example: ℗ 2002 A. B. C. Records Inc.)

19
Compilations

A compilation album is a full length record that commonly consists of fifteen or more sound recordings that share a theme or genre, each of which originates from either one or a range of record labels, artists, or bands. A single-artist/single-band theme features songs from preceding record label releases by one artist or one band only. A frequently used compilation theme is the "Best of...," "Greatest Hits," or "Singles Collection" where the best-known and most successful songs of an artist or a band are assembled in a compilation. B-side collections, unreleased tracks, or rarities are other single-artist/single-band themes that are equally released as compilations by record labels. A various-artist/various-band theme features songs by a number of artists or bands from a number of preceding record label releases covering a specific topic such as love, Christmas, hit-singles, and motion-picture soundtracks. Instead of featuring songs sharing a particular theme, a compilation can also consist of songs in a specific genre. Examples are rock, pop, jazz, reggae, hip-hop, or others.

Licenses
To physically produce and release a compilation album, several authorizations in form of licenses must be obtained by the releaser for each individual sound recording included on the "compilation" prior to it being manufactured. The releaser is the entity that finances the production and releases the album to the public. The following authorizations are necessary to orchestrate a compilation:

- The authorization from the owner of copyright in the original sound recording. The owner is usually the record company. The authorization occurs by granting the releaser a Master Use License
- A mechanical license from either the mechanical rights society or publisher, should they license directly to users, to permit reproduction of the underlying musical composition
- A song license or direct mechanical license (DML) granted by the song owner or song owners, i.e., the copyright owner in

the musical and literary works. This is a common procedure in the U.S., though not in Europe or in other countries

You should be aware that major record labels may not review requests for a planned record release if it does not exceed a minimum number of units (i.e., 10,000 or 15,000 units minimum). Compilations are not restricted to audio files only and may include many different forms of media such as video, photographs, graphic art, text, and so on. An authorization for each distinct work of art comprised in the compilation needs to be obtained by the releaser prior to its being manufactured and released. For instance, should you wish to combine a song with a video or other visuals formats, a synchronization license is also required. Interactive Compact Discs or CD-ROMs also require synchronization licenses.

License Request
To obtain a license, a license request form will have to be submitted to each party mentioned. Forms and the means of communication differ. Forms may not even exist. The information you should have handy to provide to the MRS is the precise name of the song you want to include on the compilation and applicable copyright information, the UPC barcode number of the CD you wish to use as a master, the name of your company or organization, relevant contact data, a description of your intended use of the song, the number of copies that you will be reproducing, and data regarding the forthcoming release date of your project.

Online Licensing
Certain MRSs have online song/catalogue search engines and mechanical licensing tools that simplify and speed up the process of obtaining mechanical licenses. Check with them for details. A MRS may offer a license for less than 100% of the song, since it does not administer the full copyright. You will then have to contact the other publishers of the song for the song's remaining percentage directly.

Finding Copyright Information
Information regarding the copyright owners of a song or video is specified in the copyright notice, which is printed on the booklets or inlay cards located in the cases carrying the media.

Pro-rata Computed Royalties
One of your songs may be included on a compilation. You may now ask yourself how your royalties are calculated. The answer: By using

a simple method named pro-ration. The pro-rata royalty is computed either by

- comparing the number of songs you have contributed in proportion to the total number of songs on the album *or by*
- comparing the playing time of your song in proportion to the total playing time of all songs on the album.

Using the first method: Should you have contributed one out of ten songs contained on the album, you will receive 10% of the total royalty earned (1 / 10 = 10%); should you have contributed three out of twelve songs, you will receive 25% of total royalty earned; and so on.

Using the second method: Should you have contributed one song with a playing time of five minutes out of a total of ten songs lasting sixty minutes, you will receive 8.3% of the total royalty (60 / 10 = on average 6 minutes per song; 5 / 6 = 8.33%). If your song would in contrast last six minutes, you would receive 10% (6 / 6 = 1 and 1 x 10% = 10%) of the total royalty. Should you have contributed two songs with a playing time of five and four minutes each out of a total of ten songs lasting sixty minutes, you will receive 8.3% of the total royalty for the song lasting five minutes; and 6.66% (4 / 6 = ⅔ and ⅔ x 10% = 6.66%) of the total royalty for the song lasting four minutes, thus 14.99% (15%) of total royalty for both songs.

20
Cover Songs

Definition · Licensing

A cover version is a new rendition of a previously recorded song[18]. The rights that need to be obtained to legally release cover songs are part of the publishing rights. As long as the original song is not in public domain, you must legally request permission to perform and record the music. If you intend to release a record that includes a cover, you, the licensee, are required by law to contact:

- the publisher, whether it's the author or publishing company that holds copyright ownership of the original musical work covered *or*
- the mechanical rights society, should the publisher have granted the administrative rights of the song to the MRS he is affiliated with *or*
- the Copyright Office (in the U.S. only)

Permissions must be granted prior to releasing your new version by obtaining a mechanical license. Let's look at the procedures to follow to obtain such a license in the U.S. and the U.K.:

In the United States
According to Section 115 of the U.S. Copyright Act, once a (non-dramatic) song has been released or publicly performed with the consent of the copyright owner, any person is entitled to obtain a "compulsory license" by paying the statutory fee to commercially release a cover of that song without the express permission from the copyright owner. Significant changes in lyrics or melody are not possible without the prior approval of the copyright owner in the musical and literary work. The licensee is not obligated to pay the full statutory fee to obtain a license if he can directly negotiate a better deal with the copyright owner. In case the licensee cannot directly negotiate the license fee with the publisher, he will be forced to pay the statutory fee to obtain the license.

The steps to take prior to releasing and distributing a cover record in the U.S. are thus:

1. Identify the publisher of the song
2. If the name and address of the publisher are available, contact the publisher to directly negotiate the license fee. Should the negotiations turn out successfully, proceed as agreed upon by both parties. You will quite likely still have to serve a "Notice of Intention" as is explained in point three
3. If the name and address of the publisher are available though negotiation is not an option, you can
   a. directly serve a "Notice of Intention to obtain a compulsory license for making and distributing phonorecords" on the publisher by certified or registered mail. This should happen before or within thirty days after manufacturing and before distributing any records of the cover version
   b. contact the MRS, should you receive instructions from the publisher to do so or should you find out during your copyright research that the administrative rights to the song have been granted to the MRS. Ask the MRS for further directives
4. If the name and address of the publisher are not available, negotiation is not an option, and no MRS data is provided, you will have to file a Notice of Intention to obtain a compulsory license in the Library of Congress Copyright Office.

The U.S. Copyright Office provides background information on compulsory licenses and details on how to serve a Notice of Intention in a document called Circular 73, the Compulsory License for making and distributing phonorecords. The current Web link is *http://www.copyright.gov/circs/circ73.pdf*. Another document covering this subject is named "m-200" and is available online at *http://www.copyright.gov/carp/m-200.pdf*.

Determine the total statutory fee by multiplying the number of copies to be distributed by the statutory fee per copy and send payment with each Notice of Intention. A separate Notice of Intention must be filed for each title for which a compulsory license is needed.

Cover versions can also be sold via the Internet. CDBaby, an online music distributor for independent artists, offers advice on how to legally go about releasing and selling cover versions as downloads from a Web site in the U.S. The Web page can be accessed at *http://cdbaby.net/dd-covers.* (For more on digital licensing, see Chapter Thirteen.)

In the United Kingdom
The rights that need to be obtained to legally release a cover version of a commercially published song in the U.K. are similar to those in the U.S.

You are not required to obtain the express permission directly from the copyright owner if the song has previously been released commercially. You are in contrast required to pay a mechanical license fee and obtain a license with MCPS/PRS. The license fee is fixed by MCPS/PRS and is not negotiable as is the case with the statutory fee in the U.S. You will have to complete and submit the MCPS license application with details on the cover songs to be included on the records, such as the names of the original songwriters and the copyright holders, the number of records you plan to manufacture, the retail and dealer prices of the product, the pressing plant, contact details, the artist name, and the name of the record label that will release the cover versions. Royalties are only claimed on music registered by its members. If MCPS/PRS has no claim on the songs to be released, you will receive a Notification of No Claims (NOC). A duplicate will be sent to the manufacturer.

In order to make a video or motion picture featuring this song, print and distribute sheet music, or use this song for other promotional purposes, you will also need the express permission of the publisher. The MCPS/PRS license thus pertains to audio-only record releases of cover versions. The licensee will have to pay the license fee prior to having the records manufactured. He will also have to give credit to the original authors of the songs as part of the moral rights, should the author not have waived his rights.

In order to digitally host cover versions on a Web site, the licensee will likewise have to obtain a license from MCPS/PRS.

21
Forming a Record Label

Definition ▪ Steps to Forming a Record Label

In the music industry, a record label is a brand and trademark associated with the marketing of sound recordings and music videos. A brand often includes an explicit logo, fonts, color schemes, and symbols, which are developed to represent implicit values, ideas, and even personality.[19] A brand is a symbolic embodiment of the information linked to the record label and the product it markets: the artists and their repertoire.

A record label is also the company that manages such brands and trademarks; coordinates the production, manufacturing, distribution, promotion, and enforcement of copyright protection of sound recordings and music videos; conducts A&R to find new talents; and maintains contracts with recording artists and their managers.

The term derives from and describes the round paper labels affixed to the center of gramophone records. Such labels typically contain a trademarked logo and information about the sound recording and the companies involved in creating the product.[20]

STEPS TO FORMING A LABEL
Setting up a record label entails the following steps:

1. Choose a label name
2. Set up office
3. Register your company
4. Open a business bank account
5. Insure your business
6. Organize a barcode
7. Organize an ISRC
8. Organize office operations
9. Organize promotional merchandise
10. Register with royalty collection agencies
11. Register Trademarks

We will now look at each of these steps in more detail.

1. CHOOSE A LABEL NAME

The label name you select should be unique and memorable, though should as a rule not contain offensive terms. Pick something unique because you want to establish the label's distinct brand identity and image associated with the artists and repertoire it represents and avoid any litigation resulting from trademark infringement or label, brand, or domain name disputes filed by established businesses using identical or similar names. Legal proceedings can be pricey, time-consuming, and damage the label's image you are trying to establish. You should try to prevent this by following the steps outlined below. Label names containing insulting language cannot be used in public without restraint and end up being counterproductive to your objectives. So avoid using them as well. Be creative, brainstorm, and create a short list of possible names you wish to use.

The next step is to check if each of the names is available for registration or already in use by someone else. This is a three-step process:

    1.1 Check if domain name exists
    1.2 Check if label name exists
    1.3 Check if trademark/brand name exists

1.1 Check Domain Name

If your label plans to establish an Internet presence to market and promote artists, repertoire, and merchandise online, the first and least time-consuming step is to verify if the selected name has been registered as an Internet domain name by another entity. This can be done online using the Web-based service tool "Whois" and will only take a minute or two. (See chapter 22 for further details.)

1.2 Check Label Name

To check if a label name is in use by another record company, you can consult one of the following sources:

Recording Industry Sourcebook   Music   business   and production directory updated and published annually containing more than 15,000 listings in more than sixty categories including labels, distribution, publishing, management, promotion, legal, CD/DVD manufacturing & media supply, studios, equipment manufacturing, rental and sales, art/video design and production, radio stations, venues, tradeshows and further contacts • Publisher: ArtistPro Publishing • Pages: <500 • Published since 1989 • Check for the latest edition • Price new: US$79.90, used ~US$50.00 • Purchase online or in bookstores.

Music Directory (Canada)   Extensive directory covering the Canadian Music Market containing over sixty categories including record companies, radio stations, record producers, artist contacts, music publishers and more. It also includes a schedule of events, selected discography, Canadian chart toppers, suggested reading and glossary. Publisher: ArtistPro Publishing • Pages: <500 • Published since 1989 • Check for the latest edition • Price new: US$50.00 used ~US$50.00 • Purchase online or in bookstores.

Directory (U.K.)   The simplest way to check if a label name is already registered in the U.K. is by means of a service named WebCHeck It is provided free of charge by Companies House with access to a searchable company names and address directory comprising more than two million companies. Access the Web site at *http://www.companieshouse.gov.uk/toolsToHelp/findCompanyInfo.sht ml*.

Record label directories such as *http://allrecordlabels.com*, *http://www.rlabels.com*, or *http://www.recordlabelresource.com* are also available online. An updated list of corresponding links can be found online in The Music Directory.

It is prudent to consult a number of sources when checking for label names.

1.3 Check Trademark or Brand Name
A trademark is in short a brand name and includes any word, name, symbol, or device, or any combination used in commerce to identify and distinguish the goods of one manufacturer or seller.[21] EMI, Universal and BMG are all the registered trademarks of major record companies. The label name you select constitutes a trademark in its own right once you form and start running your business and should therefore not conflict with other existing names. Here's how to avoid trademark disputes:

United States Patent and Trademark Office   You can perform an online trademark search of all trademarks registered or pending in the U.S. by using the Trademark Electronic Search System (TESS) owned and operated by the United States Patent and Trademark Office (USPTO). This is a service offered free of charge. Access the Web site at *http://www.uspto.gov*. Click on the link "Trademark *File, Search and View,*" then on the link "Search *pending and registered trademarks,*" select one of several search forms available. Input your selected name, choose "Combined Word Mark" as Field, and run a basic query. Example: Type in the name "Sun Record Company," then press "Submit Query" and see what you get.

If you intend to use a trademark that incorporates a design or logo next to your selected label name, it is advisable to perform an online design search as well. Again, you want to ascertain that your design/logo does not match an existing one that is already registered. This search will end up being more time-intensive to complete due to the complexity of the subject. Start off by selecting the search form "Free Form Search (Advanced Search)" instead of the previously used "New User Form Search." Next to "Search Term," jot down each of the components contained in your logo/design. Insert "and" between each of the terms. Choose whether each term can appear multiple times in the design by selecting "yes" or "no" next to "Plurals." Then press "Submit query." There are many other *search options* that allow you to refine your search. These are specified in the section "U.S. Trademark Field Codes." Click on each of the links to find out how they function.

You can also employ design codes when running a query. Each design or combination of designs holds a corresponding design code. These codes are equally used to register a logo or design. Start by accessing the USPTO Design Search Code Manual at *http://tess2.uspto.gov/tmdb/dscm/index.htm*, then click on the link "Introduction." Take a few minutes to read through this section. This will help as a guide to using this service. To find a list of currently used design codes in alphabetical order, click on "Alphabetic Listing." To narrow down your search, click on the link "Keyword Search."

Performing a trademark check may last ten minutes, several hours or even longer depending on the level of novelty that characterizes the name you have selected. For detailed explanations on the subject of trademarks, visit the Trademark FAQ section on the USPTO Web site at *http://www.uspto.gov/web/offices/tac/tmfaq.htm*. The information supplied includes application and registration procedures, ownership, assignment, and transferal of ownership, search, dispute procedures, and more.

The USPTO Contact Center (UCC) provides customers with general information and documents pertaining to trademarks and patents. Customer Service Representatives are available Monday through Friday (except federal holidays) from 8:30 a.m. to 8:00 p.m. U.S. Eastern Time. You can contact the USPTO Contact Center (UCC) for additional information at 800 786-9199 or 703 308-4357[22]. Further information can be found at *http://www.uspto.gov/main/faq/index.html.*

United Kingdom Patent Office   To perform a trademark search in the U.K., you can either request the Patent Office to perform a confidential search through their Search & Advisory Division. They can be reached at (++44) (0) 1633 811010. You can also conduct a basic online search using the limited text search facility available at *http://www.patent.gov.uk/tm.htm.* The Patent Office also has offices in Newport, South Wales, and London, where anyone can perform a search free of charge weekdays from 9:00 a.m. to 5:00 p.m. For any further enquiries, you can also contact the Patent Office by email at centralenquiries@patent.gov.uk.

National Patent and Trademark Offices Abroad   Every country has a national Patent and Trademark Office comparable to the one in the U.S. and the U.K. Trademarks that are registered outside the U.S. on a national, country-confined basis will not be taken into account when an online trademark check is performed using the USPTO System TESS. If your label plans to operate in a specific country outside the U.S., you should equally perform a name check with the national Patent and Trademark Office in the countries of your choice. This is a precautionary measure. Online Search Systems like TESS are also offered by other Patent and Trademark Offices.

International Patent and Trademark Search   You can also run an online check on internationally registered trademarks using the WIPO online Intellectual Property Digital Library Search Tool. Access the Web site at *http://www.wipo.int/ipdl/en*, input the name you selected, choose the database you wish to query, such as "Trademarks," and click on "Search." Choose "Design" if you want to search for registered logos and designs. This service is also offered in Spanish and French next to the English language. Further information regarding WIPO and international trademarks is also provided on the Web site. Should you find that after going through the three-step process the selected name has so far not turned up as being registered in any of the sources you checked, your label name can most likely be used and is available for registration.

You can of course consult a lawyer and have him verify this information for you. Legal fees vary, though. You may end paying up to $500 for this service.

2. SET UP YOUR OFFICE

Working from home may be a viable alternative to investing part of your money in office rent and commuting costs, especially when starting your own business. Cost savings is an important factor to keep in mind for both small and large businesses.

In many countries, running a home-based business also offers tax advantages to business owners. Trade-related expenses are frequently tax deductible. Expenses related to buildings, insurance coverage, mortgage and rent, utilities, security, phones and communications, office equipment, and more may all qualify for tax deductions. So how do you go about setting up your office? You should first check with the national Tax Authorities (Internal Revenue Service in the U.S., HM Revenue & Customs in the U.K., Finanzamt in Germany, etc.) for information regarding the business use of your home. To look at an example, check out Publication 587 published in 2005 by the Internal Revenue Service by going online at *http://www.irs.gov/pub/irs-pdf/p587.pdf*.

You should then analyze and decide if a home-based office or a detached rented or leased office space better suits your business needs. If you plan on running a recording studio from within your residence, you should pay special attention to possible restrictions relating to maximum noise levels and zoning restrictions set forth by the local government and the landlord in the rental agreement. Restrictions of use may equally apply to office space. Then write down and compare the costs of both options and weigh off what alternative works out better for you.

Should you select the home-based option, you may want to avoid using your residential address for business purposes. You can therefore establish your official business address by either renting a post office box or, should you wish a business address with a street name and number, opt for a commercial or virtual office service provider such as Mail Boxes etc. (*http://www.mbe.com*) or Regus (*http://www.regus.com*). Both offer services in the U.K. and the U.S. There are many alternative solution providers to choose from in terms of services offered and service rates charged, so it is surely worth your while to do some research online. They are available in most countries and cities. Services frequently offered are national and international mail forwarding services on a bi-weekly, weekly, or monthly basis, phone answering and forwarding services, secretarial services, and virtual office facilities with meeting rooms and office facilities that can be rented by the hour, half-day, or per day. Some services also allow company specific documents to be stored at the premises. Monthly rates charged by commercial service providers start as low as $40 per month. Renting a P.O. Box at the Post Office is a cheaper, though a less accommodating alternative. A list of commercial service providers can be found online in The Music Directory.

Should you opt for an out-of-home office space, you will have to sign an office space lease or sub-lease agreement. Lease rates vary widely and depend on a number of factors: a building's location and neighborhood, the property value, whether it is located in a metropolitan or less populated area, its appearance both inside and outside, and how well it is maintained. For more information on this subject, go online and run a search on "How to choose an office space." Be sure not to get locked into long or medium term arrangements.

3. REGISTER YOUR COMPANY
In the United States
DBA Statement
The simplest way of legally operating a business under a name other than your personal legal name in the U.S. is by filing a DBA Statement with the county clerk's office. DBA stands for "Doing Business As" and can be substituted with "Assumed Business Name," "Trade Name," or "Fictitious Business Name." In certain U.S. states and counties, the DBA statement must also be published in locally approved newspapers for a set period of time to inform the public of the business owner's intent to operate under an assumed name. The county clerk's office will give detailed instructions on what to do. Filing a DBA may take up to seven business days. The DBA Statement is generally a requirement to open a U.S. bank account and to deposit checks made out to the business. Most banks accept DBA Statements, so find a bank that does. Be sure to keep the original copy for your records in case you switch bank accounts in the future. Note that in most states DBAs do not guarantee exclusive use of a name. A business can be operated as a sole proprietorship, a Limited

Partnership (LLP), a Limited Liability Company (LLC), or a Corporation. A DBA is generally only mandatory when filing a sole proprietorship or if a business name other than the one listed on the filed articles is used. A DBA is thus not required if you file a LLC or corporation and run it using the filed name only. If you plan on using several names when running your LLC, a DBA will again be required.

A DBA and LLC are the most frequently filed legal business structures when starting a business. The basic difference between a DBA and a LLC is that the latter offers corporate protection, limiting the liability of its owners, or shareholders. A DBA in contrast does *not* protect the business owner's personal assets in case the business is sued and court judgment is entered against it for civil or financial liability. The business owners personal property, money held in personal bank accounts, equipment, or cars are at stake if the business in sued. So opting for an LLC is the safer alternative if there is property to protect. The LLC filing charges may exceed the one-time cost of DBA filing charges by $100-200, though this is a step towards being vigilant and looking ahead. Filing a DBA first and changing to a LLC at a later point is another alternative. Incorporating, or filing a "C" corporation, is another option, though a LLC most likely will suffice for your needs. Visit the Secretary of State LLC Office on the Web for additional details. Should you require further instructions on forming a LLC, go online and run a search on how to form a LLC.

Licenses & Permits
Business License   After the DBA statement has been filed, contact the local department of business assistance (licenses and permits) to verify whether or not a business license is required. A directory (categorized by state) on where to make an enquiry and whom to contact is supplied online at *http://www.sba.gov/hotlist/license.html* by the U.S. Small Business Administration (SBA). A business license is not always mandatory. Getting a business license may take up to ten business days. It may have to be renewed periodically.

Seller's Permit   You will equally need to apply for a seller's permit, also called a resale certificate, reseller's license, or sales tax license, at the State Board of Equalization, which administers the state's tax and fee programs. If your business involves selling taxable goods, wholesale or retail, or provides a taxable service, it is compulsory to obtain a seller's permit in most states before opening your business. It is currently not mandatory in the following states:

NH, AK, OR and MO. A seller's permit is a license that allows you to buy products without paying sales tax until you resell the product. For instance, selling records to a distributor. There is also an economical (i.e., cost savings) advantage in using one. Obtaining a seller's permit may take up to 10 business days. Contact the Board of Equalization in your state for details.

EIN   If your business is an employer, you are equally required to obtain an Employer Identification Number (EIN), also known as Federal Tax Identification Number. Check with the Internal Revenue Service by going online at *http://www.irs.gov*. Input the Keyword "EIN" and click on the button "Search." You will be directed to a link "Employer Identification Number (EIN)." Click on this link and you will find the necessary instructions on what to do. Sole proprietors who do not have any employees are not obligated to obtain an EIN. However, they will then have to use their Social Security number on all of their legal paperwork. Obtaining an EIN may take up to two weeks. LLCs, LLPs, and corporations also mandate an EIN. Supplementary information for small businesses and self-employed is available online at *http://www.irs.gov/businesses/small*.

SEIN   In addition, some states require an employer to obtain a State Employer Identification Number (SEIN), also known as State ID Number or Reserve Account Number. Check with the State Department of Revenue. A list of state government Web sites links is also provided on the Inland Revenue Services Internet portal.

UI   What else do you need? A State Employment Security Account Number is another requirement if you are an employer. It is based on the Unemployment Insurance (UI) Act designed to assist people who are unemployed through no fault of their own. UI is funded 100% by employers through payroll taxes. Contact the State Department of Employment Security/Labor for details.

In the United Kingdom
Registering a Company
Companies House is responsible for company registration in Great Britain. Information and guides are provided by Companies House at *http://www.companieshouse.gov.uk/infoAndGuide/companyRegistrati on.shtml*. Details on how to form and register a company are provided online. They are therefore not repeated in this guide. What form of company you may want to select is explained below.

You will also have to register for Tax and National Insurance. Registering as a self-employed sole trader with HM Revenue & Customs (HMRC) is the simplest and quickest way to start and operate a business under a name other than your personal legal name in the U.K. To do so, visit the HMRC Web site at *http://www.hmrc.gov.uk/selfemployed,* click on "Register as Self Employed," then on "Registering as self-employed for NI," and collect all data as requested in form "cwf1." Then call up the help line for the newly self-employed at (++44) 08459 154515 and register by phone, which is the quickest alternative. You can also print out the form and send it to the address stipulated in the form or drop it off at any U.K. HMRC Office.

You will have to decide if you want to register for VAT. VAT is a tax that applies to most business transactions involving the transfer of goods or services. VAT registration is not mandatory if your supplied taxable goods and services do not exceed £61,000 over a one-year period or if you anticipate supplying taxable goods and services to amount to more than £61,000 in the next thirty-day period alone. Instructions regarding Value Added Tax (VAT) registration as well as National Insurance (NI) registration are provided on the HMRC Web site. NI registration is, however, mandatory, though payment can be postponed should the business not earn any income in the initial period of operation. If you are planning on taking on one or more employees, you must call the New Employer's Helpline at (++44) 0845 6070143 for instructions on what to do.

Limited Companies
You can also opt for a different legal business structure such as a Limited Liability Company (Limited), Limited Liability Partnership (LLP), or partnership. As does a U.S. LLC or corporation, a Limited protects the shareholder's personal assets in case legal judgement is entered against the business. A U.K. Limited is comparable to the U.S. corporation (not the LLC). There are three basic types of limited companies: private company limited by shares, public company limited by shares, and private company limited by guarantee. The private company limited by shares is more often selected by people starting a business due to the simplicity of setting it up. To operate this type of company, a minimum of two directors, of whom one can act as the company secretary, and a registered office in England or Wales are mandatory. English or Scottish law applies.

Capital is raised by selling shares to investors. The authorized share capital—the maximum amount of shares you can issue to investors—must be determined when forming the company. It can be as low as £100 (i.e., 100 ordinary shares of £1), though normally is set at £1,000. It is possible to change it at a later point in time in accordance with the Articles of Association. A minimum of one share must be issued, which is done by means of allotment to at least one shareholder when forming a company. This is the money you are required to pay up to legally form your company. A private limited can have one single shareholder only. Shares can be sold and share certificates transferred to other investors. A Limited calls for dealing with administrative duties throughout the year. Examples are filing Form G88(2) when allotting shares, maintaining statutory books, delivering annual returns and filing annual accounts, overseeing and managing taxation issues, preparing and filing written resolutions, holding shareholder meetings, and more. Running a Limited means allocating some of your time to dealing with these matters.

Small Business Service (SBS), an executive agency of the U.K. Department of Trade and Industry, provides a clearly structured Internet gateway with all the necessary facts on how to choose the legal structure of your business, how to set it up, and where to register. The Web site address is *http://www.businesslink.gov.uk*. For anyone starting a business in the U.K., this Web site will surely be of great use. Be sure to click on the links "Business names & structures," "VAT," "PAYE and National Insurance," and "Your type of business" and follow the instructions. Key regulations and licenses that apply to your specific business categories will be supplied. Companies House provides at-source information at *http://www.companieshouse.gov.uk*, as does HMRC (Tax Authorities) at *http://www.hmrc.gov.uk*. Published literature is equally available. For beginners, check out "Do-it-yourself Limited Company" (*http://www.lawpack.co.uk*), an easy to understand, clearly structured guide explaining the basics with examples of forms in the back section. Needless to say, there are many other books worth looking at.

Online Company Formation Agents can assist you in setting up a U.K. Limited Company. The standard service is available for as low as £35 (plus 17.5% VAT) and consists of assisting you in completing and filing the Memorandum of Association, Articles of Association, and Forms 10 and 12 at Companies House, which are required by law to form and register a Limited in the U.K. Additional services may comprise access to online systems that allow clients to file forms such as the Annual Return (Form 363a), Change of Accounting Reference Date (225), and Change of company officers (288) once the Limited company has been successfully registered. Note that Companies House equally has an online system available free of charge to directors and company secretaries that accomplishes the same task. To use this service, a separate registration with Companies House is necessary.

4. OPEN A BUSINESS BANK ACCOUNT

In order to open a business bank account as sole proprietor, a U.S.-based LLC or Corporation, or a U.K.-based Limited, you will need to provide the following documents to the bank:

- An account opening mandate from the bank
- Details of the business and business activities you plan to run
- Details of where the seed capital to start the business has come from
- A driving license, ID, or passport
- Social Security number or Tax ID Number (U.S. only)
- Recent utility bill stating your current home address
- Physical or registered address of business
- A list of the persons who can sign on the bank account and a sample of their signature
- Certificate of incorporation for limited companies
- DBA Statement (U.S. only)
- Minutes from Board Meeting (U.S. Corporation only)
- Check, money order, or currency to cover initial cost and first deposit

When comparing banking offers, you should pay attention to the following: Bank charges and fees (get a list of all charges including periodical fees, money transfer charges national and international, check books, etc.) and compare them ▪ Opening hours ▪ Telephone and online banking facilities ▪ Interest rates and savings options ▪ Borrowing facilities ▪ Merchant services ▪ Company credit card ▪ Introductory offers for new customers such as free business banking for the first twelve or eighteen months, free banking card with no annual fee in the first year, free help to plan starting your business, free small business software, etc.

For further facts on U.K. bank accounts, go online at *http://www.businesslink.gov.uk*, click on the link "Finance and grants," then on "Business banking."

5. INSURE YOUR BUSINESS

When starting a record label, you may want to consider the following insurance coverage: Property, Liability, Theft, Fire, Medical/Dental, Life, and Worker's Compensation. For music professionals, this can include coverage for: Musical Instruments and Equipment • Automobile • Building • Studio Liability • Tour Liability • Medical/Dental • Travel and Personal Accident • Public Liability • Employee Disability • Long-term Care/Disability • Key man Life Insurance • Employment Practices Liability (EPLI) • Professional Liability • Business Interruption • and Renter's Insurance. Employee Fidelity Bond (Protection against Employee Theft) and Umbrella (Additional Liability Protection) are possible add-ons.

Certain insurance coverage is required by law if you have employees. In the U.S., the Worker's Compensation Insurance is mandatory by law. It provides coverage to employees who are injured while on the job. In the U.K., the Employers' Liability Insurance is compulsory by law. It is comparable to the U.S. Worker's Compensation Insurance. Ask an insurance agent for further details and rates. Professional Liability Insurance protects business owners against financial losses from lawsuits filed against them by their clients. Employment Practices Liability provides protection for an employer against claims made by employees, including former and potential employees. It covers discrimination, sexual harassment, wrongful termination of employment, and other employment-related allegations linked to the company, its directors, and officers. Key man Life Insurance is a coverage linked to critical employees or artists that are key to the company's operation and its success.

A number of companies specialize in providing insurance coverage for music businesses and professionals. Some equally provide special insurance coverage packages for self-employed and small businesses. Music Pro (*http://www.musicproinsurance.com*) as well as The Actors Fund (*http://www.actorsfund.org*) and NASE (http://www.nase.org) are examples of insurance service agents in the U.S. Music Guard (*http://www.musicguard.co.uk*), La Playa (*http://www.laplaya.co.uk*) and Victor C. Knight (*http://www.victorckni*

ght.com) are examples of insurance providers in the U.K. You can also visit the Insurance Information Institute's Web site at *http://www.iii.org* for general information on insurance types and policies in the U.S. The Incorporated Society of Musicians (*http://www.ism.org*) and Musicians Union (*http://www.musiciansunion .org.uk*) offer free public liability insurance (up to £10m) to its members in the U.K. Links to other insurers (categorized by country) are supplied online in The Music Directory. Consult several insurance agents or insurance companies and start comparing the rates and coverage offered.

6. ORGANIZE A BARCODE

Barcodes are placed on commercial products and used by most companies to track and control their sales and product orders once they are nationally or globally distributed and sold in retail stores. They are symbols commonly printed on the back of a product in the shape of a white-colored rectangle containing patterns of black vertical bars with spaces and numbers placed below the bars. Barcodes are readable through scanner devices. The numbers are encoded in the symbol and uniquely identify each product. GS1 globally supplies these barcodes to businesses. Take a look at the back of this book for an example of a barcode.

Background   GS1 is a worldwide network currently comprising 133 national member organizations (GS1 Partners) with a system (the GS1 System formally known as the EAN-UCC System) used by one million companies doing business in over 140 countries across 23 industries. Each GS1 Partner provides supply chain standards and key technologies to businesses in order for them to efficiently and globally manage information regarding their products, assets, services, and global locations. Bar-coding in GS1 Standards includes the following four key supply chain technologies: Bar-coding; Electronic business messaging; Radio frequency identification; and Data synchronization.

Whom to contact   To obtain a barcode, a company has to contact the GS1 Partner in the country it is registered. Should you have formed your label as a LLC in the U.S., you will have to contact GS1 U.S.. Should you have set up your label as a Limited Company in the U.K., you will need to contact GS1 U.K. For companies headquartered in France, GS1 France is the partner to contact. And so on. You'll find a detailed list containing contact and Web site information of all the GS1 partners listed by country in alphabetical order at *http://www.ean-int.org/contact/worldwide.php.*

6.1   For Companies in the United States and Canada
In the U.S. and in Canada, the 12-digit UPC (Universal Product Code) barcode, also referred to as the UPC-A barcode, is generally used.

Barcode/GTIN   The barcode contains a group of digits positioned below the bars that is called the Global Trade Item Number (GTIN). It consists of a company prefix, an item reference number, and a check digit.

Membership Application   In order for companies registered in the U.S. to obtain a license to use and print UPC barcodes, the company will first need to become a GS1 U.S. Partner Connections member. Membership is administered by the Uniform Code Council which is now part of GS1 U.S.. A membership application can be completed and submitted online by accessing the GS1 U.S. Web site at https://catalog.webec.uc-council.org/create_account.cfm.

Membership Fee   An initial fee and an annual membership fee will need to be paid before your membership is approved. This amount is dependant upon your company's annual turnover, or in the case of start-up companies expected turnover, and the number of unique products to be identified. As a rule: The more unique products your company intends to sell, the higher the fee. For a record label starting off with several artists signed to the label and several releases planned for the upcoming year, the minimum fee should apply.

According to the current 2006 GS1 Fee Schedule, the minimum initial fee, for a total of 100 products to be identified with a unique barcode, is $750 with an annual renewal fee of $150. An additional charge based on the company's existing or projected gross annual revenue may also be charged. As start-up companies struggle to pay these high amounts in their first years of operation, changes in fees and fee structures may be implemented in the near future. Contact GS1 for an exact quote.

By the way   Companies who became members of UCC (now GS1) before August 28, 2002, are not obligated to pay membership renewal fees to UCC to maintain membership as a condition for their use of Company Prefixes issued to them by UCC, or as a condition for Basic Membership Benefits as defined in a Class Settlement

Agreement (*http://www.ibcaweb.org/ucc-settlement.htm*). Check with GS1 for further details.

Creating your Barcode   When your membership is approved, your company will receive a membership kit with a letter of authenticity containing the unique company's identification number called the company prefix. The prefix number is variable in length dependent on the number of the company's unique products and consists of six, seven, or eight digits. You will then have to assign a number (Item Reference Number) to each of your individual products in order for them to be uniquely identifiable. You will finish creating the GTIN by adding the check digit, a number calculated from the Company Prefix and Item Reference Number, using a calculator or the formula provided by GS1. Detailed instructions on the procedures are included in the membership kit. GS1 will also be able to help out by email or phone in case you have any questions.

Printing your barcode   When you have your GTIN in hand, you will need to decide how the barcodes will be printed and applied to your products. There are several approaches. Contact a printing company that simply prints the barcode labels that you can then apply to your product; contact a printing company that will print the barcode directly on the package of your product; or print the barcode labels or barcode as part of your CD/DVD booklet yourself using off-the-shelf software. GS1 U.S. provides a Solutions Center to GS1 U.S. Partner members providing guidelines on creating and printing UPC barcodes, the barcode standards, a list of barcode printers, a barcode consultants directory, and more. However, be aware that GS1 itself in general does not provide barcode design or production software.

Contact GS1 U.S.   You can contact the GS1 U.S. Partner Connections team Monday thru Friday 8:00 a.m. to 8:00 p.m. U.S. Eastern Time at 1-937-435-3870. You can also contact them via email at info@gs1us.org.

6.2   For companies outside the U.S. and Canada
EAN Code   GS1 issues a different barcode type, the EAN (EAN-13 or European Article Numbering system which is also called JAN in Japan) code, to companies that are registered outside the U.S. and Canada. It is generally a 13-digit barcode equivalent to the 12-digit UPC barcode used in the U.S.

EAN vs. UPC Since GS1 announced that, starting January 1, 2005, all retail scanning systems in the U.S. must be able to accept the EAN-13 next to the standard UPC symbol, both barcode types can be used on a worldwide basis. This change eliminates the need for companies who export goods to the U.S. and Canada to double-label their products, which was necessary prior to 2005 and more expensive for those involved. The U.S. has equally started the process of shifting toward the EAN-13 symbol, which will be known as the UPC-13 symbol. This is good news for companies that trade globally and simplifies the application procedures as well.

Membership Application The membership application and barcode (GTIN) creation procedures are very similar to the ones explained in the previous pages. Access the GS1 Web site of the country your company is registered and follow the instructions.

Membership Fees Fees vary considerably by country. The best thing to do is to get a quote from GS1 in your country of registration. To give one example: The minimum initial GS1 U.K. joining fee is £94 and the annual subscription fee is equally £94. Including the obligatory Value Added Tax (VAT), the total annual cost comes to £221 (US$380) in the first year and a minimum of £110 (US$190) in the years thereafter. This is a considerable difference from the fee charged by GS1 U.S. Whether this will change is not clear.

6.3   Getting a barcode or not
If you are planning to sell your products through distributors or directly to record stores, barcodes are essential. Not only are they useful to track and control sales and product orders, but the sales data provided by retail stores to Soundscan is also used by Billboard to generate the retail music sales charts. Many radio stations in the U.S. also use barcodes to generate their daily play lists. And many distributors and record stores may not consider your CD without a barcode. So if you are serious about marketing your CDs or DVDs through traditional retail channels, apply for membership at GS1.

7. ORGANIZE AN ISRC
The International Standard Recording Code (ISRC) provides[23] a means of uniquely identifying sound recordings (SR) and music videos internationally. It does not, however, identify physical products such as audio carriers or audiovisual carriers, which are identified using barcodes. Any entity creating sound recordings can obtain an

ISRC. Membership with an industry association or other organization is not required. The ISRC is free of charge.

The first owner of the rights to a recording normally assigns the ISRC. It identifies the recording throughout its life and is intended for use by owners of sound recordings and music videos, as well as by copyright organizations, broadcasting organizations, chart companies such as the U.K. Charts Company, libraries, and licensees. The ISRC has been developed in order to globally facilitate the accurate exchange of information on the ownership, the use of recordings, and the administration of corresponding rights.

The ISRC is alphanumeric using digits and letters and is constructed as follows: Country Code (2 digits) - Registrant Code (3 characters) - Year of Reference Code (2 digits) - Designation Code (5 digits). The Registrant Code is provided by the ISRC agency and is forwarded to the applicant after his request has been received. The other digits are composed by the applicant personally. Detailed instructions on how to construct an ISRC and encode it in digital sound carriers are available in the ISRC handbook by going online at *http://www.ifpi.org/isrc/isrc_ handbook.html*.

Contact ISRC   To obtain an ISRC, contact the ISRC agency, which is appointed by IFPI, in your country. A list of national ISRC agencies is provided online at *http://www.ifpi.org/isrc/isrc_agencies.html*.

8. ORGANIZE OFFICE OPERATIONS
Here is a short list of additional things you should arrange prior to commencing with the operation of your record label. Most of these points are self-explanatory, so no further comments are added:

- Office equipment required: Telephone, fax, printer, scanner, and computer
- Office software that may be required: Word processing; accounting, invoicing & tax; graphic art; and CRM (customer relationship management) software
- Organize studio and sound recording equipment and software
- Set up a business office and cellular phone and fax line
- Set up a professional voice mail messaging service
- Register Internet domain
- Design professional Web site

- Find an accountant, preferably a certified public accountant, and discuss initial steps of operation

9. ORGANIZE PROMOTIONAL MERCHANDISE

Design and manufacture record label related representational and promotional merchandise:

- Design record label logo, which is reproducible in a variety of sizes in digital as well as physical form
- Design business cards, mailing/shipping labels, stationary, and invoices
- Design promotional merchandise for your record label, such as t-shirts, key-rings, coffee mugs, etc.
- Contact local and national printers and request quotes for the services they provide. Determine best offer. Get initial quantity of selected items and promotional merchandise manufactured. Check quality of products. Use this as test for future jobs linked to record releases

10. REGISTER WITH ROYALTY COLLECTING SOCIETIES

Record labels that are about to release records to the public have to affiliate with royalty collecting societies. The works to be released must then be registered with these societies.

11. REGISTER TRADEMARKS

At some point, a record label may want to secure exclusive rights to its logo, name/word, or slogan. This is feasible by means of trademark registration. A registered trademark protects a name, word, and logo within a specified service and product area and gives the trademark owner the exclusive rights of use in the territories where the trademark has been registered. This undertaking is not inexpensive, so it only makes sense to contemplate trademark registration if a business is likely to be around for a while.

In the United Kingdom

To register a trademark in the U.K., you need to submit the application Form TM3 to the Patent Office. Fees currently start at £200 covering registration of a logo or name under one class. £50 is charged for each additional class. Detailed information on trademarks, including booklets on specific topics, is available on the U.K. Patent Office Web site at *http://www.patent.gov.uk/tm.htm*. It includes instructions on how to register a trademark, fees, forms, benefits, international registration, and contact data. You can also consult a trademark attorney who is legally and professionally qualified in trademark matters. A directory of attorneys is provided by the Institute of Trade Mark Attorneys. Visit their Web site at *http://www.itma.org.uk*.

In the United States
You can use the Trademark Electronic Application System (TEAS) available at *http://www.uspto.gov/teas/index.html* to file a U.S. trademark application directly over the Internet. Filing fees are summarized on the Web page "USPTO Fee Information" available online at *http://www.uspto.gov/web/offices/ac/qs/ope*. Fees start at $300, $150 for small entities. You can also mail or hand deliver a paper application to the USPTO. You can call the USPTO's automated telephone line at (800) 786-9199 to obtain a printed form. Further details relating to Trademark registration is provided online at *http://www.uspto.gov/go/tac/doc/basic/howtofile.htm*. In depth factual information is available at *http://www.uspto.gov/go/tac/doc/basic*. A directory of U.S. Trade Mark Attorneys is available on the Find Law Web site at http://lawyers.findlaw.com/lawyer/practice/Trademarks.

International Patent and Trademark Registration
Trademarks can also be registered internationally with the International Bureau of the World Property Intellectual Organization (WIPO). By filing a single application called the "International Application," a trademark can be registered and secured in any of the countries that have joined the Madrid Protocol. Details can be found on the WIPO Web site at *http://www.wipo.int/trademarks/en*. National trademark offices may also be able to help you out. The U.S. and the U.K. have both joined the Madrid Protocol. Instructions on how to file an application is also supplied online. The filing fee is a combination of a basic administrative fee next to an individual per country, per class fee. The filing fee is thus contingent on the number and selection of countries and the number of service or product classes selected. For details relating to filing fees, visit the Web page at *http://www.wipo.int/madrid/en/fees/about_fees.html*. A fee schedule and calculator are both available. Fees are indicated in Swiss Francs. One Swiss Franc is currently around $0.80US and £0.43. For background on trademarks, go online to *http://www.wipo.int/about-ip/en/trademarks.html*. Contact information is equally available.

Before filing an International Application, you should verify with WIPO that no additional charges from national trademark offices are required when registering.

Another possibility to register trademarks internationally is through the Office of the European Union Trade Marks and Design (OAMI). However, registration is limited to EU member states only. These currently include Poland, the Netherlands, Belgium, Luxembourg, France, Spain, Germany, Austria, Italy, Sweden, Finland, Denmark, the U.K., and Ireland. A number of new member states have joined the EU in 2004 and several other countries are scheduled to join in 2007. They will be integrated over time and trademark registration in these countries will also be possible using the CTM (Community Trade Mark) application procedure provided by OAMI. All questions relating to Trademark registration and fees are available on the OAMI Web site at *http://oami.europa.eu/en/mark/marque/question.htm*. Further details are available online at *http://oami.europa.eu/en*. What advantages OAMI has compared to WIPO is not apparent, however.

With all the foundational knowledge of how things work, you are ready to take the steps to forming a record label.

RUNNING YOUR LABEL

You can now start focusing on a record label's main task, which may encompass finding and signing artists/bands to your label, arranging for the development and production of their music, planning, manufacturing, packaging, distributing, releasing and promoting their records, administering finances and royalties, coaching artists/bands prior to a record release, arranging public performances (life gigs, life tours, radio, TV, and Internet appearances, interviews with the press), marketing the artists/bands on a local, national, or international basis, and assisting the artists with their personal needs. This equally includes connecting with the industry players, such as manufacturers, distributors, retailers, broadcast media, and promoters.

22
Domain Registration

**Domain Name System ▪ Domain Name ▪
Domain Type ▪ Registrar ▪ ISP ▪ Whois ▪ ICANN**

Although domain registration is an IT specific subject, I have included some background information on how it functions so your research is limited to checking which domain names and domain types are available for registration. For those familiar with registering a domain, skip this chapter.

What is the domain name system and what is a domain name?
The Domain Name System (DNS) helps users find their way around the Internet. Every computer on the Internet has a unique address called its "IP address" (Internet Protocol address). Because IP addresses, which are strings of numbers, are hard to remember, the DNS allows a familiar string of letters, the "domain name," to be used instead. To give an example: Rather than typing "192.0.34.163," you can type www.icann.org.[24] Both lead to the same Internet destination when typing them into to your Internet browser. In this example, "icann" is the domain name and ".org" is the domain type, also referred to as the domain extension or domain suffix. When registering the label's domain name, you will also have to select at least one domain type.

What are domain types?
There are two types of top-level domains: generic and country code. Both are mainly used by companies and persons when registering. There is an additional special top-level domain (.arpa) for Internet infrastructure. Generic domains were created for use by the Internet public, while country code domains were created to be used by individual countries as they deemed necessary.

Here are some examples:

- Country Code Domains (.uk, .de, .jp, .us, de, fr, etc.)

- Generic Domains (.aero, .biz, .cat, .com, .coop, .edu, .gov, .info, .jobs, .mobi, .int, .mil, .museum, .name, .net, .org, .pro, .travel, .tv, etc.)
- Infrastructure Domain (.arpa)

The most extensively used generic domain type is ".com." It stands for commercial and is suitable for commercial sites only. ".org" stands for organization and defines non-profit organizations. ".net" stands for network. It is growing in popularity, as is ".info" and ".tv." Certain domain types are restricted to particular user groups or countries; others are available to all users. Check with your Internet Service Provider (ISP), which is the company that enables you to connect to the Internet, or check with one of the numerous registrars for a complete list of domain types that are currently available. Further information relating to domain types can be found online at *http://www.iana.org/domain-names.htm*.

What does it mean to register a domain?

The Internet Domain Name System (DNS) consists of a directory of all the domain names and their corresponding computers registered to particular companies and persons using the Internet. When you register a domain name it will be associated with the computer on the Internet that you designate during the period of registration. Internet users around the world will then be able to access your domain.

How do I register a domain name?

Domain names can be registered through many different companies known as "registrars." There are numerous registrar services. You should also check if your ISP is able to act as a registrar. Most ISPs offer this service.

The registrar you choose will ask you to provide contact and technical information when registering. The registrar will then keep records of the contact information and submit the technical information to a central directory known as the "registry." This registry provides the data to other computers on the Internet and enables data exchange between each of them. You will also be required to sign a registration contract with the registrar, which sets forth the terms under which your registration is accepted and will be maintained.[25]

How to check if a domain name is available for registration?

You can check this online by using a Web-based service tool called "Whois." It is a *TCP/IP*-based query response protocol which is widely used for querying a database in order to determine the owner of a domain name, an IP address, or an autonomous system number on the Internet. And it is simple to use. This service is free of charge. Do not pay for it. Many registrars offer the Web-based tool on their Web sites. Try using the following online service tool at *http://news.nic.com/cgi-bin/whois*. Feel free to use "Whois" on any other Web site where available.

Then type in the selected domain name and domain type. For example, enter sunsetrecords.com if you want your label name to be Sunset Records and have chosen .com as the domain type, and click on "Submit Query." Should the domain name and domain type be registered to someone else, details of the registrant will be specified. You will then have to select a new domain name and domain type and try again until you are successful.

If you are planning to offer music or products in a particular country, you may also want to consider registering country-specific domain types that are connected to the domain name you have selected. Continuing with our previous example, sunsetrecords.us for the U.S., sunsetrecords.de for Germany, sunsetrecords.jp for Japan, or sunsetrecords.co.uk for the U.K.. Whether additional domain type registration is necessary depends on the size and objectives of your business. You should check with your ISP or a registrar for existing domain types and related costs. Every individual domain type that is registered will be at an additional charge.

How much does a domain name registration cost?

Each registrar sets the price it charges for registering names and prices vary significantly among different registrars. An annual, quarterly, or monthly fee may be charged. Some registrars offer discounted or free registration services in connection with other offerings, such as Web hosting. You should therefore check with several registrars including your own ISP and visit their Web sites to compare prices. Do some research and find out what offer best meets your needs.

What do you buy when registering a domain name?

You are buying the right to use a domain name and a domain type for a specified period of time and the right to renew it at the end of that period.

What is ICANN?

ICANN, the Internet Corporation for Assigned Names and Numbers, is an internationally organized, non-profit corporation that has responsibility for Internet Protocol (IP) address space allocation, as well as protocol identifier assignment, generic (gTLD) and country code (ccTLD) Top-Level Domain name system management and root server system management functions.

23
The Music Retail and Online Market

**Media ▪ Retail Channels ▪ Business Models ▪
Music Retailers ▪ The Global Market ▪ Market Share ▪ Music
Retailers ▪ Digital Music Services ▪ Research Companies ▪ RIA**

The music industry retail market can be analyzed by examining and differentiating between the media that is sold and the retail distribution channels through which this is done.

Media
Physical media includes CDs, Dual Discs, vinyl, and other multi-channel music formats. Digital media includes music and video download and streaming, cellular phone ringtones and ringback tones, and digital sales through retail kiosks.

Retail Channels
A music retailer can choose one or several of the following retail channels to sell his media to the public. He can either:

- sell physical media at a traditional store or point of sales (i.e., a record store, supermarket, grocery store, warehouse, drugstore, at concerts, etc.)
- sell physical media online to be delivered to the customer by mail
- sell digital media online to be delivered by digital means through streaming or download to computers, PDAs, mobile phones, or other digital devices

Business Models for Digital Media
The business models for digital media currently used by online music retailers include:

- the "à la carte" download per song or album model where customers can buy one or more tracks on a per track or per album basis. The music can be downloaded to a computer hard drive and can be copied to CDs, portable music players, computers, mobiles, or other digital devices

- the subscription model where customers pay a monthly flat fee and are able to download a specified number of songs per month to any digital device. eMusic, for instance, charges $9.99 a month for 40 songs and $14.99 for 65 songs
- the streaming model, such as the one used by the U.S. Service RealNetworks' Rhapsody, where customers pay a monthly flat fee and then have unlimited access and can listen to a provider's complete repertoire by means of streaming. This is similar to a subscription based model with one major difference—downloading a song to any digital device is charged extra, usually for under a dollar per download

Some online music stores offer a choice of two models—streaming and downloading—to its customers. Ringtones are generally sold to customers using the download model. Providers may offer a variety of models in the future. The trend is clear: more music is licensed and distributed through a rising number of digital distribution channels and file formats to a growing number of customers.

Music Retailers

Music retailers that sell digital media online can be classified into several groups:

- Traditional retail, predominantly chain, stores that sell music through their online portals next to the traditional retail channels. Examples are Wal-Mart, Target, Circuit City, and Borders.
- Record Labels that directly sell music and merchandising products of artists signed to the labels via their own proprietary online stores to customers. Examples are Sony Connect, Sony Music Store, Virgin Digital, Virgin Megastores, and V2
- Digital-only online music stores that operate independently

Each of the independent digital retailers is required to sign a license agreement with the record labels or distributors to get permission to market and sell their music online.

The Global Market

According to figures released[26] in the first quarter of 2006 by the International Federation of the Phonographic Industry (IFPI), the global recorded music sales of physical and digital media to retailers and distributors in 2005 fell by 3% to $21 billion compared to 2004. Global sales revenues of physical media fell by 6.7%.

The Digital Music Report 2006[27], equally published by IFPI each year, shows that record company trade revenues from worldwide digital sales almost tripled in value, from $380 million in 2004 to $1.1 billion in 2005. Digital sales in 2005 accounted for approximately 6% of the recording industry's global worldwide revenues based on the first six months of the year.

Online and mobile music distribution globally emerged as the industry's fastest growing delivery channels, with an estimated split of 50/50 between online and mobile music distribution, though with wide deviations among regions and countries. As IFPI reports, mobile distribution dominated the digital music market in Japan and parts of continental Europe, while online sales were relatively stronger in markets such as the U.S., the U.K., and Germany.

The number of legitimate music download sites has also increased from 50 in 2004 to 335 in 2005. Digital music distribution is continuing to spread internationally.

Music Markets
The top ten music markets, based on global sales of physical and digital media, in declining order during 2005 were: USA, Japan, United Kingdom, Germany, France, Canada, Australia, Italy, Spain, and Brazil.

The U.S. is clearly the largest single market worldwide, with the U.S. recording industry accounting for slightly more than one-third (35–37%) of the world market. Japan is and continues to be the second dominating market and holds by and large 16% of the total market, followed by the U.K. and Germany, each accounting for between 7 and 9%. Mexico, Switzerland, Russia, Belgium, South Africa, Sweden, Austria, Norway, and Denmark are the markets that take in places ten through twenty in terms of market size for the year 2005. The top twenty music markets made up around 90% of the global music market in 2005.

The top ten digital markets, based on global sales, in declining order in 2005 were: USA, Japan, U.K., Germany, France, Italy, Canada, South Korea, Australia, and the Netherlands.

Market Share

The music market is dominated by the "big four" or "majors" record companies, which, according to data published by IFPI, hold 71.6% of the market share worldwide. Universal Music Group maintained its position as the world's biggest recording company for the year 2005 with a 25.5% share of the world market. Sony BMG Music Entertainment was next with a 21.5% share, followed by EMI Group at 13.4%, and Warner Music Group at 11.3%. The independent sector held the remaining 28.4% of global share.

Nielsen Soundscan figures differ, with Warner Music Group ahead of EMI in third position and the independent labels accounting for only 18% of market share instead of the 28% as was reported by IFPI. Nielsen SoundScan reported that the big four accounted for 81.87% of the world music market in 2005, Universal Music Group 31.71%, Sony BMG Music Entertainment 25.61% (13.83% Sony, 11.78% BMG), Warner Music Group 15%, EMI Group 9.55%, and the independent labels 18.13%. The exact truth lies somewhere in these numbers.

The U.S. Market

Let's briefly look at the U.S. numbers covering 2005. The overall music industry sales in the U.S. fell slightly by 0.6% to $12.27 billion. The overall sales figures have decreased every year since 2000, except for 2004 when sales increased by 4.1%. 1999 was the best year over the last decade, when sales peaked at $14.59 billion.

According to the 2005 music industry sales numbers, listed by segment,[28] provided by the Record Industry Association of America (RIAA), sales of physical media fell by 7.9% to $11.2 billion. The combined U.S. 2005 revenues for digital media retail sales were $1.07 billion. Sales through digital downloads, however, still accounted for less than 5% of total revenue.

For those interested in exact U.S. figures: Revenues from single song and album downloads grew by 174.5% to $503.6 million. The figure includes a modest $3.7 million in music video downloads; kiosk sales accounted for only $1 million. They were not tracked in 2004, so no comparison of revenues is available. Sales of 170 million ringtones and ringbacks generated $421.6 million in consumer sales. Sales numbers were equally not tracked in 2004 by the RIAA, so no comparable numbers are available. In 2005, 1.3 million consumers subscribed to subscription-download services in the U.S., generating $149.2 million in revenue for download services.[29]

As these numbers show, legal digital music retailing is continuing to grow in popularity. This trend is also confirmed by other record industry associations around the world and by research companies such as Forrester Research and Jupiter Research. Whether digital sales will compensate for lost CD sales in the future remains to be seen. The "digital revolution" opens up new possibilities for unsigned artists to market their songs to a larger community at home and abroad. How artist or bands can distribute their songs to leading online music stores and what criteria they should reflect on before signing up will be explained later in this chapter.

Major Music Retailers in the U.S.
According to the NPD Group, the top ten music retailers, based on the equivalent number of units sold[30], in the third quarter of 2005 in the U.S. were as follows:

Wal-Mart (discount retailer) · Best Buy (discount retailer) · Target (mass merchandiser) · Amazon (world's largest online retailer) · FYE · Circuit City · Apple/iTunes · Tower Records · Sam Goody (Musicland) · Borders

Each of these companies (except for Apple/iTunes) sell music as physical and digital media though traditional *and* digital distribution channels. Next to the companies just listed, there are many other competitors that also earn money selling music using both distribution channels: Barnes & Noble, Kmart (online discount retailer), Bluelight (online discount retailer), or J&R Music are examples. The list is non-exhaustive. There are many other worthy independently run music retailers that equally offer online music stores in the U.S. However, the ones listed here and on the following pages are at present the major players reaching the highest number of customers in the U.S.

Digital Music Services in the U.S.
Apple's iTunes Music Store is the only company in the top ten list of music retailers to be solely based on digital rather than combined sales. According to NPD, more than 7 out of 10 U.S. digital music sales made via the Internet (for the third quarter of 2005) were through iTunes. Apple's iTunes is currently the most successful online music store worldwide. So who is directly competing with Apple's iTunes for a piece of the online digital music retailing pie? Apart from

the major retailers listed above, here's a list of some of the leading legitimate digital online music stores (service providers) in the U.S.:

AOL Music · Artistdirect · Beatport · BuyMusicHere (Muze) · ClearChannel · CDNow · Cdigix · **101 CD** · CD Universe · Click2Music (BMG Music) · **Connect (Sony)** · Ebay · EMD · Emusic · Fox Music · FYE · Grazemusic · **HMV** · Indieburn · Instavid (Warner Music Group) · LifewayStores · mMode · **MP3.com** (CNET Networks) · MP3tunes · Mperia · **MSN Music** · **MTV** · Musica360 · MusicGiants · MusicMatch (Yahoo!) · MusicNet · MusicNow (AOL) · **MyCokeMusic** · **Napster 2.0** · PassAlong · Peer Impact (Wurld Media) · PureTracks · Rhapsody (RealNetwork) · **RealPlayer (RealNetworks)** · **Sony Music** · **SoundBuzz** · Soundtouch · Streamwaves · TVTRecords · **Virgin Digital** · **Virgin Mega** · **V2** · Urge · VoyMusic · WarnerBrosRecords · WhatsTheDownload · **Yahoo! Music**

Check The Music Directory for corresponding Web links. The above list is again non-exhaustive. It includes record companies that digitally market and sell music—the works of bands and solo artists signed to their labels—directly to customers using their proprietary Web sites, as well as independent digital music services that have signed license agreements with and market music on behalf of major and independent labels.

Territory

A growing number of online music retailers provide their services on an international basis. The names highlighted in bold letters in the preceding list are services that currently operate in countries outside the U.S. Customers can thus use these shops in a variety of countries depending on where they reside. iTunes, for example, has extended its service to currently twenty-one countries. Soundbuzz at present operates in thirteen countries, currently dominating the Asian market. MSN Music is at present the third largest retailer in the Europe. HMV, MTV, Virgin, My Coke Music, Napster, and many others are also expanding. Needless to say, some online services are limited to one country only.

Digital Music Services outside the U.S.

A list of the current major digital music services to be found online for the five largest music markets, besides the U.S., is provided below. It includes both nationally and internationally operating services:

Japan
Excite
Itunes Japan
Kandora
Label Gate
Listen Music Store
Love Music Store
Mora
MSN Music Japan
Music.jp
OCN Music Store
Oricon Style
Ongen
Reco-Choku
Yahoo! Music

U.K.
Bleep.com
Connect (Sony) UK
CD Wow! Wow Tunes
Daily Express
Daily Snack
Daily Star
DJ Download.com
easyMusic.com
HearItBuyItBurnIt.com
HMV Digital
iTunes UK
Karma Download
Loot Tunes
MetroTunes
Ministry of Sound
MSN Music
MTV UK
MusicRadio.com
Mycokemusic.com
Napster UK
Nervous Records
OK Magazine
Panasonic Music Stream
Packard Bell UK
Peoplesound
PlayLouder
Rough Trade
Sonic Selector

7Digital
Streets Online (Woolworth)
The Hut
Tesco
TuneTribe
Virgin Digital UK
Vitaminic Music Club UK
Orange UK
War Child Music
Wippit UK
Woolworths

Germany
AOL Musik Downloads
Connect Germany
FHM Music (via Musicload)
Finetunes
Freenet
Hotvision
Independent Dance
iTunes Germany
Kontor
Magix Music Shop
Mediamarkt
Media Online
Medion Music
mp3.de (not MP3.com)
MSN Music Club Germany
MTV Digital Downloads
Germany
Musicload (Nr. 1 in Germany)
Napster
One4Music
Packard Bell Germany
RTL Musik (via Musikload)
Saturn
Tiscali Germany
WOM

France
Alapage
Belgacom
Connect (Sony) France
Cora Music

E-Compil
Fnac
iTunes France
M6Music
MSN Music France
MTV Digital Downloads
France
NC Numericable
Packard Bell France
Skynet
Tiscali France (Alice)
Virgin Megastore France
Orange France

Canada
Archambauktzik
Bonfire at Futureshop
iTunes Canada
Napster 2.0 Canada
Puretracks
Sympatico

Australia
BigPondMusic
CD Wow Biz
ChaosMusic
D-Store
HMV Australia
iTunes
JB Hi-Fi
MP3.com
Mulemusic
NineMSN
Ozmusicweed
Play4me
Sanity
7digital
Soundbuzz

List compiled August 2006

Web links (i.e., Internet addresses, URLs) to each of these services can be found in the Pro-Music Worldwide Directory. They are also catalogued in The Music Directory.

Worldwide Directory
The most complete listing of all major digital music retailers is made available online in the Pro-Music worldwide directory of authorized digital music services (listed by country). You can access the directory online at *http://www.pro-music.org/musiconline.htm*. The

directory is updated regularly, though services may have disappeared prior to having completed the latest updates. A listing of Web sites where physical music products can be ordered online is also provided on the Pro-Music Web site by clicking on the link "Retailers and Etailers listing."

Major Music Retailers outside the U.S.

To complete our overview of the music market, let us look at the major retail stores in the five largest music markets next to the U.S.: In Japan, these are HMV, Virgin Megastore, Tower Records, Disk Union, and RECOfan. In the U.K., these are HMV, Virgin, Virgin Mega, and MVC. In Germany, the leading retail stores are Saturn, Media Markt, and Kaufhof (all part of the Metro Goup Holding), as well as Medimax, Pro Markt/Makro Markt, EP, and Karstadt. And in France, they are Fnac (part of the Pinault-Printemps-Redoute Group), Virgin Megastores, Carrefour, Géant, Leclerc, Monoprix, Auchan, and Printemps-Haussmann.

Ringtones

Cellular phone ringtones and ringback tones are marketed through independent providers of mobile content and entertainment services, as well as through the cell phone companies themselves. Examples of providers who primarily specialize on mobile content are Jamster, Flycell, Zingy, RingtoneJukebox, BlueFrogMobile, and GSMonline to name a few. The number of services alike will continue to increase. Digital music providers may end up breaking into this market segment as well. AOL Mobile is such an example. Examples of cellular phone companies selling ringtones directly to customers are O2, Vodafone, T-Com, Orange, Cingular, and Verizon. There are of course many more.

Comparing Online Music Stores

When comparing online music stores, there are a range of criteria to look at. This may be interesting for consumers who seek a convenient and consumer-friendly shopping experience, but also for independent artists who are reflecting on where to place their songs online. Here are the main criteria to consider:

Number of claimed songs in repertoire · Number of genres to choose from · Number of claimed customers · Online business models (download and/or subscription) · Pricing for downloads per track, per album or as a monthly subscription fee · Portable player support (proprietary such as Apple's iPod or non-proprietary to be used for several file formats) • Software download required to use service and if so, is the software Web-based or computer-based? • Compatible operating systems (OS) and browser support for music services provided • Digital Rights Management (DRM) technology (yes/no) • Burn options (number of times a song can be exported, copied or burned onto portable players, computers, CDs or other digital devices • File format (mp3, wma, acc, real, or other) • Bitrates of downloads (64 kBit/s, 128kBit/s, 192 kBit/s, 256 kBit/s, etc.) • Pre-Listening (in Bit rates and seconds) • Number of clicks to download • Replacement for damaged or lost downloaded files • Rebates • Mode of payment (Credit Card, Firstgate, Premium SMS, Pay-Pal, check, or other) • Special Features (charts, exclusives, promotional tools, ad-free radio stations, news, newsletters, specials, tips) and DMA support.

Research Companies
The names NPD, Nielsen Soundscan, and Forrester Research are quoted on several pages in this guide. The names apply to research companies that track, collect, and analyze data for particular markets and industry segments. A list of additional research companies that concentrate on the music market is provided below:

- The NPD Group tracks music sales in the U.S. The ranking information is sourced from NPD MusicWatch, a monthly tracking study of consumer music purchases and NPD MusicWatch Digital, a monthly panel reporting digital music acquisition provided by the NPD Group. *http://www.npd.com.*
- Nielsen Soundscan tracks sales of music and music video products throughout the United States and Canada. Sales data from point-of-sale cash registers is collected weekly from over 14,000 retail, mass merchant, and non-traditional outlets. Nielsen SoundScan is also the sales source for the Billboard music charts. *http://www.soundscan.com.*
- Hitwise Research globally tracks and compares leading Web sites in over 160 niche industry categories. *http://www.hitwise. com.*
- Forrester Research is a technology and market research company that provides advice on technology's impact on business and consumers. *http://www.forrester.com.*
- Jupiter Research helps customers plan digital music strategies through online consumer and teen surveys and detailed customer segmentation analysis

- Gartner Media Research focuses on helping customers develop new strategies to capitalize on behavioral and technological changes. *http://www.gartner.com.*

Next to record industry associations, these and other research firms act as a key source for valuable information sought after by individuals and companies servicing and competing in the music industry. Research data is, in general, available for purchase on request. Bits and pieces of this data are also available for free in articles, online, in the print media, or on TV.

Record Industry Associations

Nearly every country has a national record industry association (RIA), a trade group that represents the national recording industry. Its members are record companies and distributors. In other words, those companies create, manufacture, and distribute most of the sound recordings in their homeland. Their tasks in general terms can be defined as protecting intellectual property rights worldwide and the rights of artists, conducting consumer industry and technical research, and monitoring and reviewing state and federal laws, regulations, and policies[31]. Keep in mind that the RIAs do not represent the interests of authors. Assessments and conclusions may not always be in favor of the artists.

A list of record industry associations sorted by country is provided online by IFPI. The Web page is accessible at: *http://www.ifpi.org/con tent/section_links/national_associations.html.* Annual and quarterly reports published by each trade group are sources of information for companies servicing the music industry. Additionally, RIN (Recording Industry in Numbers) is the most complete source of music industry statistics worldwide covering sixty-five music markets in sixty-five countries and is published by IFPI and available for purchase. Find further information online by visiting the Web page at *http://www.ifpi.org* for details.

Independent Artists

As an independent artist, band, or record label with music to market, you will be looking for ways to get your songs distributed to online retail outlets in order for new customers or a growing fan-base to have access to, listen to, and eventually purchase the works of art. How can you achieve this? You can either use an online music distribution services to assist you with this task or decide to directly affiliate with online music retailers. Let's look at both options now.

24
Online Music Distribution

**Definition • OMD Compensation •
OMD versus OMS • OMD Contracts •
OMDs in the Market Place • Downside of OMDs**

One way of selling your own music to the public is by using an online music distribution (OMD) service that will act as middleman and distribute your songs to numerous retail outlets, including major digital music download and subscription services (DMS), online CD retailers, and traditional CD retailers. The OMDs encode and normally encrypt the digital audio files you forward to them prior to distributing them to the retail outlets or the licensees. They act as the centralized contact for all digital distribution needs on behalf of its members. This includes negotiating standardized agreements and licensing rates with existing and new digital music retailers, controlling and making monthly royalty payments, and organizing marketing programs to increase label brand awareness.

OMD Compensation
The OMD may charge a setup fee on a per-Album/CD release basis or on a per-song basis next to deducting a service fee or commission rate, which is a percentage of the total income made through each retail outlet that is affiliated with the OMD. However, business models vary. Some OMDs charge a commission and no setup fee, some charge no commission but a setup fee on per-song basis, and some charge a commission and a setup fee on a per-CD release basis.

To clarify this point: On a "per-song basis" means that the OMD charges a one-time fee for every song that is released, encoded, encrypted, and distributed to music retailers. On a "per-CD release basis" means that the OMD charges a one-time fee for the total number of songs contained on a CD that are released and distributed to music retailers. For a CD Album, this is normally between ten and thirteen songs. Per-song setup fees are currently around $15 and per CD release setup fees are between $30 and US$40. The commission rate currently charged by the majority of OMDs is 30% or less.

The income passed on by the OMSs to the OMDs and thus to its members includes earnings from the sales of digital downloads of songs and ringtones, from subscriptions that enable customers to stream the OMS's total repertoire or download a maximum number of songs from the OMS's repertoire, or from physical CD sales to the public that are ordered through the OMSs. OMDs are currently expanding their services by delivering CDs into physical CD stores through affiliations with major national distributors as well. However, there are restrictions in placing songs of unsigned artists in stores, as we shall see when looking at CDBaby.

OMD versus OMS

An online music distributor (OMD) should not be confused with an online music store (OMS), also called online music retailer (OMR). An OMS engages in marketing, promoting, and selling music directly to the end-consumers. They are also not to be mixed up with promotional sites for bands or artists who are seeking to be signed to record labels, record labels proprietary online stores, or A&R services, webzines, or other marketing and promotional resources available online. Before scrutinizing several leading OMDs, there is one important point I will touch on first: OMD Contracts.

OMD Contracts

Read through and understand the terms and conditions stipulated in your contract drawn up by the OMD prior to agreeing to it. When signing an agreement with an OMD or OMS, you should pay attention to the aspects listed below. Signing an agreement in most cases simply means clicking on the button "Yes, I have read the terms and conditions and agree to what is stated within". More and more OMDs will be competing for a slice of the distribution market, so comparing contracts and shopping for a better deal is advisable. Don't sign away your rights without thinking twice about the consequences of being bound to these legal clauses once your CD sales or song downloads start taking off. Selling music is clearly a business. And being prudent is part of running a business. Let's take a look at the most important details to keep an eye on before signing such an agreement.

Grants ▪ Licenses ▪ Rights ▪ Jurisdiction

- Do not sign a contract if you are not holder of all of the copyrights of the works you intend to market through the OMD. The contract contains a warranty that affirms that you are the copyright holder of the works, also referred to by the

OMD as the authorized content. You will be held liable should a copyright infringement lawsuit be brought in court due to your breach of warranty.

- Do not assign your copyright in the sound recording to the OMD/OMS. Instead, grant a license to the OMD/OMS to simply use the sound recordings. In other words, you should retain full ownership of and rights to your sound recordings.

- Limit the form of distribution of your songs to commonly used means and technologies. These are currently digital downloads of songs and ringtones to phones, PDAs, and computers as well as physical distribution by mail order. New forms of distribution or transmission should be on an approval-only basis. This is a difficult point to fight for. Contracts ever so often contain phrases like "but not limited to" or "including, without limitation," which broaden the playing field of the OMDs immensely and which they will be reluctant to erase from the contract. Check your contract for such wordings.

- Specific licenses should be granted to the OMD on an approval-only basis. Relevant examples are the synch license, the license to use one or more of the songs as promo tracks that are generally exempt from royalty payments, the license to include a song in a compilation, or the license to use a song as part of the OMD's advertising campaign. Your contract should not automatically grant these rights to the OMD, except of course if you agree to this point.

- Your contract will be governed by and disputes decided according to state or country law. This is generally the law of the state or country where the OMD is legally registered. Any claims must be brought forward in the courts of that state.

Term

- The term of a contract should be limited in time, ideally short-term. Be sure to verify that your contract includes a termination clause. This clause allows *you* to terminate the agreement upon handing in a written notice, typically after thirty days, where all the rights you granted to the OMD will be reversed back to you. This should be stipulated explicitly in your contact. If not, ask for details. No other conditions should be attached to this right of termination. You do not want to be bound to a long-term contract without having the option to end it. Watch out for words equal or similar to "perpetual," "permanent," or "continuous" when the term of an agreement is defined. This is an important point.

- The contract should be non-exclusive to avoid limiting your means of marketing, distributing, and selling your song elsewhere.

Compensation ▪ Royalties

- Compare the setup fees and service fees charged by the OMDs. Most contracts spell out that the artists are responsible for any royalties owed to publishers, songwriters, or producers, which must hence be paid out of their share of the income. This is common practice.

- The contract should assert the right to you to affiliate with a performance rights society and any other entity that monitors, collects, or pays out royalties to you for the public performance of your songs and sound recordings.

- Free downloads, such as promo tracks, are based on the concept of free goods and are royalty-free. The artist generally earns no money from free downloads or streamings. You could nevertheless try to seek compensation for this type of use from OMDs or OMSs, as they are benefiting from your music. On the other hand, it helps to promote your song. You could limit the number of free downloads to a set quantity or time frame.

Accounting ▪ Audits ▪ Transparency

- The contract should specify that the OMD accounts for and pays royalties owed to the artist or label on a monthly or quarterly basis. You should have the right to object to royalty statements and to audit the books and records relating to the sales of your sound recordings. Independent Auditing Firms or royalty collecting societies can audit a record label or OMD. The term to object should extend over several years.

- OMDs in general provide regular statistics on songs or ringtones that are sold by means of download or streaming and for which the artist or label gets paid. These statistics do not, however, include downloads and streamings for which they are not paid. Knowing how often a royalty-free promo track has been played or a pre-listening streaming link has been clicked on is valuable information to the copyright owner. The statistics provided by OMDs should include this data. Verify with the OMD what information is included.

To put it quite bluntly and in simple terms, let's imagine that ten downloads were made, though you get paid for only five out of ten. Five instead of ten therefore show up on your account statement. You do not know that ten downloads were made in the first place. Information has been withheld. When and for what purpose were the other five downloads actioned? Were they used as free goods? You obviously don't know. So there still remains work to be done until we can talk about transparency in the digital music business, especially from the point of view of an author or band marketing and selling songs via these distribution channels. The statistics provided to you may not be a real measure of control.

In the U.S., Soundscan and SoundExchange may assist artists and authors in monitoring what songs are played online. Visit the Web sites at *http://www.soundscan.com* and *http://www.soundexchange.com* for further details.

OMDs in the Market Place

So what companies offer this type of service? Let's look at two major OMDs and examine the cost and benefit for artists or bands who are thinking of joining:

- CDBaby *http://cdbaby.net*
  Based in the U.S. • Setup Fee for worldwide digital and/or physical distribution of each new CD release: $35. • No annual fee • Service Fee: Deducts 9% from all income paid out by the music retailers. • Deducts $4 for every CD physically sold through your Web page on the CDBaby Web site • Pays its members one week after revenues are passed on by music retailers • Distributes to major online music retailers, including iTunes, Napster, MSN Music, Sony Connect, etc. as well as to a growing number of mobile content providers • In-store

distribution (with focus on U.S. stores) is also available, though placement of your CDs in a store will only happen if requested by a customer • You can opt to release your song via digital means only (excluding physical distribution) • A UPC Barcode is supplied for a $20 charge per release and an ISRC Code is supplied free of charge • Registers your release with Soundscan • You must be holder of the copyright in the sound recordings you release • The agreement you sign with CDBaby is non-exclusive. • It has a 30-day termination clause for both parties, after which you have the right to request your music to be withdrawn from the retail outlets • Pay attention to the optional rights you grant to CDBaby in case you sign up: The more rights you confer, the lesser your degree of control of your songs. You may, however, gain more publicity by spreading the word, so you need to weigh off what is more important to you. Optional rights are currently linked to promo tracks and synchronization rights.

- The Orchard *http://www.theorchard.com/thedeal/index.php*
Based in the U.S. • Setup Fee for worldwide digital distribution of each new CD release: $49; Setup Fee for worldwide digital and physical distribution of each new CD release: $99. Discounts are available for multiple simultaneous releases • No annual fee • Service Fee: Deducts 30% from all income paid out by the music retailers. The Orchard equally deducts added expenses related to shipping and inventory management from income. • Pays its members on a quarterly or bi-annual basis. Variations apply. Check payment details on their Web site • Distributes to major online music retailers including iTunes, Napster, MSN Music, Sony Connect and others. • In-store distribution (same proceedings as with CDBaby) • A UPC Barcode is automatically supplied for free for each album release. An ISRC Code is equally supplied free of charge • Registers each album release with Soundscan • You must be holder of the copyright in the sound recordings you release • The agreement you sign with The Orchard is non-exclusive • It includes a termination clause. The termination request, however, has to be approved by The Orchard. On what grounds the request could be denied is not specified, nor is it explicitly stipulated that you have the right to request your music to be withdrawn from the retail outlets. • Pay attention to the rights you grant to The Orchard: You may be obligated to sign an agreement that grants The Orchard

"perpetual non-exclusive distribution rights to your music." Perpetual means forever and implies that you will have less or no control over what happens to the songs you submitted to the OMD in the long run, even after you terminate your agreement. It is advisable to clarify these points with The Orchard management prior to signing an agreement.

Explanations: The word "income" used in the previous two pages is equal to the wholesale price, that is the price at which your CD/Album or song is sold to the OMSs.

Next to CDBaby and The Orchard, there are a growing number of other online music distributors. As already mentioned, some of these services are based on different business models. IODA, for example, charges no setup fee per song or album, but takes a percentage of each sale. TuneCore charges its members a one-time per song per store setup fee, though passes on all of the revenues paid out by the music retailers to its members. Some OMDs provide additional services that focus on digital marketing and promotional music licensing, including blog and podcast promotion. So it may be time well spent to compare the services and business models offered by different OMDs and contact them, should information be missing. Here are several other OMDs that may also be of interest to you:

- IODA *http://www.iodalliance.com*
  Based in the U.S. • No Setup Fee • Service Fee: Deducts 15% from all income paid out by the music retailers • No annual fee • Pays its members on a monthly basis • Distributes to major online music retailers including iTunes, Napster, MSN Music, Sony Connect, etc. as well as to a growing number of mobile content providers • A UPC Barcode is supplied for a $25 charge per release and an ISRC Code is supplied free of charge • You must be holder of the copyright in the sound recordings you release • The agreement you sign with IODA is non-exclusive. • IODA has a 90-day termination clause.

- TuneCore *http://www.tunecore.com*
  Based in the U.S. • Setup Fee: $0.99 per song per store; Annual maintenance fee: $7.98 per album release (regardless of the number of songs the album contains; an EP or single is also considered an album) • No service fee and no commission charged on income • A la carte OMS selector: Members can select the online stores and country (e.g.,

iTunes U.S., iTunes Japan, etc.) his/her songs are to be delivered to. • Pays its members as soon as revenues are passed on by music retailers • Distributes to a growing number of major online music retailers including iTunes, Sony Connect, Rhapsody U.S., eMusic U.S., etc. • A UPC Barcode and/or a ISRC Code are supplied free of charge • You must be holder of the copyright in the sound recordings you release • The agreement you sign with TuneCore is non-exclusive. • Termination by written notice per album per store is possible for a $20 fee.

- I AM Music Online *http://www.iammusiconline.com*
  Based in the U.S. • Setup Fee for worldwide digital distribution of each new CD release: $49 • No annual fee • Service Fee: Deducts 30% from all income paid out by the music retailers • Pays its members on a quarterly basis • Distributes to major online music retailers including iTunes, MSN Music, Napster, MusicNow, Sony Connect, etc. as well as to a number of mobile content providers • In-store distribution not available • A UPC Barcode and/or a ISRC Code is supplied for a $50 charge • You must be holder of the copyright in the sound recordings you release • The agreement you sign with I AM Music Online is exclusive (no other OMD can be used for digital distribution) • You have a 90-day termination clause. It is not explicitly stipulated that you have the right to request your music to be withdrawn from the retail outlets. Check this with management prior to signing an agreement.

And some other OMSs (though without further comments):

- Digital Rights Agency *http://digitalrightsagency.com*
- Iris Distribution *http://www.irisdistribution.com*
- IDEA *http://www.ideadistributors.com*
- Zebralution (for labels only) *http://www.zebralution.com*
- Digital Pressure (for labels only) *http://digitalpressure.com*
- INGrooves *http://www.ingrooves.com*
- The Can (Australia) *http://www.thecan.com.au*

Do note that this list again is non-exhaustive. Many OMDs are based in the U.S., though are accessible to users from around the world. You do not necessarily have to reside in the U.S. to be able to sign up for membership with the OMDs. New services will without doubt pop up in the future. Check The Music Directory for new OMDs.

Downside of OMDs
Although this may change in the future, you should be aware that most OMDs still distribute your songs to *all* online retailers the OMD is affiliated with. You will therefore not be able to select or directly communicate with the retail outlets that best suit your needs. Services are starting to turn up that allow its members to be more selective and choose from a list of OMSs and countries they operate in. TuneCore is such an example.

OMDs do not enable you to individually negotiate the terms and conditions of the agreement you will be signing, control the exact timing your release is to be scheduled (it takes between three weeks and four months to get your works placed in an OMS and you cannot control when this happens), or select the territory where this will occur, the file format in which your songs are to be delivered to the customer, and the Digital Rights Management policy you wish to implement to secure digital content when selling your sound recordings to the public. For independent artists or labels promoting their artists, this may cause some headache. Whether direct contact with individual OMSs brings about better results remains to be seen.

What it comes down to is a loss of control of the effective handling of the artist's music, including decisions regarding placement, type of use, marketing and promotion, once a song or an album is released. This is done in exchange for mass exposure and a cutback in time spent dealing with research, negotiation, administration, and legal issues. And there is one thing to remember: the majority of leading OMSs still do not license music directly from unsigned artists, which in the end is a convincing argument for many to use OMDs in the first place. There are a lot of benefits that OMDs offer to independent labels and artists compared to times in the past when major record companies had a stronghold on the music industry as a whole. It is a matter of deciding what it is that you want to achieve.

25
Online Music Services for Artists

Selecting an OMS · List of OMSs · Social Networking Online · Selling Downloads from Web Sites

Next to using online music distributors to spread the word and promote and sell your works to the public, you can also go direct by contacting and signing agreements with online music stores or digital music services that license music directly from unsigned artists or independent labels. A number of online music stores promote and sell songs of superstars alongside those of independent artists. As part of their service, OMSs in general provide a shopping portal to the public, including a secure shopping cart to handle fraud protection, turnkey order processing, complete credit card or payment processing, online administration tools for artists, shipping and handling of customer orders, promotional tools, and more.

Selecting an OMS
Criteria to look at when selecting the OMS you are intending to affiliate with are listed as follows: Pay-per-CD sold to be physically distributed (yes/no) · Pay-per-download service to be digitally distributed (yes/no) · A la carte or subscription service based on digital downloads sold and/or streamings (yes/no) · Cost to member (monthly or annual fee, set-up fee, service fee/commission rate, or other fees such as shipping, packaging, inventory or product return costs) · Sign-up procedure · Time it takes to sign up · Approval requirements · *Regarding digital (online) content*: Media storage space available: 5, 10, 20MB or more · Number of songs you can upload (limited/unlimited) · Formats supported (mp3, wma, acc, etc.) · Quality of downloads indicated in bitrate offered to customers: 128, 192, 256 or 320 kBits/sec · Is DRM (Digital Rights Management) supported to secure digital content (i.e., your songs – yes/no) · Soundscan registration and reporting (yes/no) · Streaming or download of sample audio or video clips and length of clips (yes/no) · Free and customizable artist page (yes/no) · Quality, design, and layout of Web site · Total number of songs in OMS repertoire · Total number of songs sold by OMS · Total number of bands/artists that are signed up to OMS · Total number of bands/artists that sign up to

(or get approved by) OMS each month • Are songs from major artists also marketed and sold via the OMS • Special promotional features: blogs and podcasts, band's/artist's private message board, mailing list, newsletter, discussion forums, gig calendar, customer reviews added to band/artist page, music charts, background radio, cross-promotional tools, etc. • Is copyright assigned or granted as a license to the OMS • Payment of earnings to members: Monthly/Quarterly • Worldwide or national distribution available • Non-exclusive or exclusive agreement • Termination clause: 30, 60 or 90 days • Affiliate programs with other services.

There are numerous online music stores out on the Web; however, few of them offer all of the features listed above. You therefore need to take a closer look at what is and what is not included in the deal before signing up for membership. Let's look at two online music stores more closely that market and sell songs by independent artists and bands to a worldwide audience:

- Amazon.com *http://www.amazon.com*
  The "Advantage Program" is a "Pay-per-CD sold" promotion and physical distribution program for independent musicians. • *No* digital Pay-per-download or subscription program is available. • Annual fee for residents of or companies located in the U.S., Canada and Mexico: $29.95. Commission rate: 55% deducted (by Amazon) from the suggested retail price, which is set by its members. No further deductions are applied if your CD is sold (at some point) at discount. • A membership application must be filled out and submitted online. • The application procedure lasts between two and three weeks on average. • A UPC bar code, residency or a company registration in one of the three countries mentioned, and the ownership of copyright in the works are a requisite to join the program. • You may offer a limited number of free mp3 downloads as a promotional tool to customers through the Digital Music Network. • Advantage program in the U.K.: Membership costs £23.50 (including VAT) per year; Commission rate: 70% of dealer price. Requirements: Residency or company registration in the U.K.; registration with Redmuze (redmuze.com); EAN-13 Code • Amazon offers similar Advantage programs depending on the country you reside or your company is located in. Program names may vary. Advantage Premium, Professional, or Marketplace Programs offering different fees and commission rates are

also available. Check with Amazon nationally for details. •
DVDs, Videos and books can also be sold via Amazon • Free
stocking, shipping to customer, customer service, and cover
scanning is included in the deal • Earnings though sales are
paid out on a monthly basis. • Full access to your sales,
inventory, and payment reports is available. • Worldwide
distribution of your music to customers. • Leading platform
where independent and major artists market and sell their
products. • The agreement with Amazon is non-exclusive with
a 30-day termination clause.

- Indie Store *http://www.indiestore.com*
  (Part of 7Digital Media Ltd.; an OMS located in the U.K.)
  Pay per download service (songs and ringtones) only • A la
  carte digital download service • No annual fee or set-up fee if
  you select the Starter Service; Commission Rate: 70%
  revenue share, quarterly accounting • Annual fee for the Pro
  Service (upgrade): £75; No set-up fee; Commission Rate:
  80% revenue share, monthly accounting. • Complete and
  submit application form online • Time it takes to sign up: 1
  hour • Number of songs to upload: 4 (Starter Service); 20 (Pro
  Service) • Formats supported: AAC (iPod) , WMA and MP3
  files at 192kbps (or above) • DRM: Yes; available upon
  request by member: (a) Store one copy of the downloaded
  music track on up to five personal computers; (b) Store one
  copy of the downloaded music track on up to five portable
  personal digital content players; and (c) Make up to ten copies
  of the Music Track on CD-ROM or other physical media. •
  Upload of up to four tracks (Starter Service) and up to 20 (Pro
  version) possible • Download samples sound clips are
  available for every song sold • Free artist page: yes;
  professional look • Markets songs of major artists (through
  7digital) and independent artists (through Indie Store) •
  Special features: URL, track previews, blog, photo gallery,
  events calendar; artist mailing lists and personal forum are in
  planning • Additional features for Pro Service: Promotion on
  the 7 Digital network; Chart eligibility in U.S., U.K. and 20
  other countries; ISRC generation (should you not have one) •
  Distribution Rights are licensed (not assigned) to 7Digital. You
  retain the rights to your music • Worldwide digital distribution
  available • Non-exclusive agreement • Termination clause:
  one year (check if your works can be withdrawn from their

Web site beforehand should you decide on terminating the agreement before the period is over).

List of OMSs

The two online music stores are meant as illustrations. It is beyond the scope of this book to analyze each OMS currently offering similar services. The preceding pages should help analyze what to focus on when selecting the OMS you want to sign up with. Here is a non-exhaustive list of OMSs you may want to check out:

Amazing CDs *http://www.amazingcds.com* Artistopia *http://www.artistopia.com* ArtistGigs *http://artistgigs.com* Audigist *http://www.audigist.com* AudioLunchbox *http://www.audiolunchbox.com* AudioPyro *http://www.mediapyro.com* AudioStreet *http://www.audiostreet.net* BroadJam *http://www.broadjam.com* Backstage Commerce *http://www.backstagecommerce.com* Besonic *http://www.besonic.com* Garage Band *http://www.garageband.com* Isound *http://www.isound.com* Lulu *http://www.lulu.com* Mperia *http://www.mperia.com*	MP3Powered *http://www.mp3powered.com* MusicDock *http://www.musicdock.net* MusicGorilla *http://www.musicgorilla.com* My Own Music *http://www.myownmusic.de* No. 1 Band *http://www.number1band.com* OEBase *http://www.oebase.com* Primetones *http://www.primetones.com* Overplay *http://www.overplay.com* Peoplesound *http://www.peoplesound.com* Soundclick *http://www.soundclick.com* Real Music Community (Real Networks) *http://uk.real.com/guide/community* *Promotional* Download.com (CNet Networks) *http://music.download.com* MP3.com (CNet Networks) *http://www.mp3.com/signup/artist*

Downloads.com and mp3.com are mainly used for promotional purposes. You cannot directly sell any music via these sites to the public; however, links to OMSs are available from within. Both providers include chart services, offer songs to a potentially worldwide fan base, put links to the artists' or bands' main site, and publicize them internationally.

Social Networking Online

Social Networking Web sites are used increasingly in a variety of industries, including the music industry. They are dedicated to the development of thousands of unsigned acts. Independent artists and bands use these sites to promote their works and to find an online following. They join a growing community of like-minded people to connect, share information, exchange opinions, and join forces to collaborate on new projects. These sites are used as a vehicle for new acts to emerge, build a fan-base, and become more popular without having to rely on record companies or publishers to release their material. The most popular networking sites, such as myspace.com, are equally being used by artists signed to major labels. Social Networking Sites include individual Web pages of artists, bands, or producers with audio and video streaming and download facilities to showcase their songs, blogs, photos, news stories, gig calendar, and links to their main Web sites. Using these sites is presently free of charge. If downloads are sold via these sites, the income is generally split in the band/artists' favor while retaining all rights to their music. Artists and bands should consider networking sites to promote themselves and their songs.

Here is a list of some of the leading networking sites:

- Artist Now *http://www.artistnow.com*
- My Space *http://www.myspace.com*
- Pure Volume *http://www.purevolume.com*
- You Tube *http://www.youtube.com*
- Eyespot *http://eyespot.com*
- Flagr *http://www.flagr.com*
- Facebook *http://www.facebook.com*
- Revver *http://www.revver.com*
- Our Media *http://www.ourmedia.org*
- Second Life *http://www.secondlife.com*

Selling Downloads from Web Sites

Artists and bands also have the option to sell their songs directly from their Web sites to the public by means of digital downloads. A growing number of service providers are offering easy-to-integrate vendor solutions for existing Web sites, enabling sellers and buyers to complete secure transactions. Customers who visit the Web site and decide to purchase a song simply click on a download link and fill out their payment information. Customers can use major credit cards and other payment systems such as PayPal or FirstGate to purchase and download songs. The transaction is securely verified online via the service provider and when approved, the download begins. The seller can generally track when, where, by whom, and how often a song has been downloaded. Income is periodically transferred to a designated bank account, usually on a monthly basis. Server space is provided to upload songs to secure servers. Added features that may also be available are song-file management tools, account management tools, Digital Rights Management Tools, several file formats supported (mp3, wma, acc, etc.), image galleries, and more. Some services even offer ready-to-use Web site templates with integrated vendor solutions, so designing a Web site is not a requisite to selling music from your Web site. Service providers may charge a one-time set up fee, a monthly fee, and/or a commission rate on the revenues made from downloads sold. Commission rates vary, though seldom exceed 30%. Producers, publishers, managers, or anybody else who wants to sell music from a Web site can also use this approach. Overall, this solution provides a bigger degree of control to the seller, with an equal or better payout of income made per download compared to OMSs. Artists and bands should consider using this alternative alongside OMSs to sell their songs online.

Here are several service providers:

- Musicane *https://www.musicane.com*
- MediaSphere *http://www.entriq.com*
- Payloadz *http://payloadz.com*
- Navio *http://www.navio.com*
- 2Checkout *http://www.2checkout.com*
- Backstage Commerce *http://www.backstagecommerce.com*

Further Listings
What else can you sell? Sure, merchandise. There are numerous stores online that assist artists and bands in doing so. And I could continue filling these pages with names of interesting sites. What have I done instead? Visit The Music Directory, where you will find a directory with links sorted by category and country related to the music industry. The directory is updated regularly and new providers will be added as they come along. In the last section of this chapter we'll focus on songwriters and how the Internet can be of use to them. So keep on reading.

26
Selling Songs as a Songwriter

Selling Songs to Performing Artists ▪ List of Services

Selling Songs to Performing Artists

Digital services that assist songwriters who are seeking leads and contact information to A&R (Artist & Repertoire) departments of record labels or production companies in marketing their songs to established or new-coming performing artists are also available online. The services are generally subscription-based where members sign up for a period of six months or one year to have online access to regularly updated listings that include a per song/per project description of the genre/style and theme of music sought after, the name of the performing artist who is looking, the deadline by which songs must be submitted in order to be considered, and the means and format by which songs should be forwarded to the people in charge next to the relevant contact data. A directory of music industry professionals by name and company is equally provided by several services. Interviews with successful A&Rs, news with regard to the music business, and information on how to improve your songwriting and better market your songs are also published on a regular basis.

Although each service provider surely has its success stories, you should be aware that placing a song with a superstar or established artist is more the exception than the rule for most members. Many successful A&R Managers primarily in the U.S. do not accept unsolicited material. So even if you have the relevant contact details, this may still not be of any help in getting your song on their desks for consideration. A list of 500 names consisting of some of the leading players in the music industry, their phone numbers, and address details sounds pretty impressive. Though what is the purpose if these players are a) not using the service you have signed up for to look for new material and b) do not accept unsolicited material. As you will see, these services cost a fair amount of money.

So here's a personal note to those thinking of signing up for membership: Prior to signing up, try to examine if your songs have some degree of marketability. Ask yourself how many of the artists you know could perform your song. Ask yourself what makes your song great, the chorus, chord progression, beat, tempo, originality, etc., and imagine listening to it on the radio, the Web or on TV. Can you? Be objective and get some professional feedback, should this be possible. In a way, this sounds dreadful. Music should come from your heart and should be accepted as such. That is true. But the thing is, you are writing for other performing artists and not for yourself. In fact, you are writing for the market and creating music on demand. And your song must therefore match the request to get a chance of being selected. So before paying several hundred dollars in membership fees, be sure to think this over.

List of Online Services
Here is a list of services assisting songwriters in finding listings/leads of songs music industry professionals are looking for. These services are in alphabetical order. Evaluate the advantages and disadvantages of each individual service prior to selecting one.

- Cuesheet *http://www.cuesheet.net*
  Bulletin listing projects for film and TV productions and other media projects based primarily in the U.S., Canada, the U.K., or Ireland • The listing is dispatched twice a month by e-mail only • Subscription-based service • Subscription Rate: 3 months: £150/US$234.00; 1 year: £495.55/US$773.00 • Cuesheet is part of Songlink International (see below).

- Music2deal.com *http://www.music2deal.com*
  Music2deal incorporates 3 (previously separate) forums: Songs2Deal, Artist2Deal and Vocals2Deal. • Songs2Deal is a portal where songwriters and music publishers exhibit their works • Artist2Deal is a portal where bands and projects are being showcased to the world • Vocals2Deal is a portal where voices are presented to producers • You can currently sign up as an artist or vocalist to exhibit your music or vocal tracks to parties seeking new material • Music2deal.com facilitates a direct contact between professionals in the music business worldwide and cooperates with partners in six territories (GSA, Scandinavia, Benelux, Italy, U.K., USA). In the Benelux, Songservice.com represents music2deal. • Subscription-based • Annual Subscription Rate: Artist Membership including three songs that can be showcased, each of them can be exchanged for no additional charge + Email:

US$59.95; Vocal Membership: same deal, however pertaining to vocal tracks: US$29.95 • Other rates and discounts are available • Service is based in Germany, though operates internationally.

- Songlink International *http://www.songlink.com*
  English bulletin with listings/leads of artists or bands in search of songs • Primary markets with highest success rates: Germany, Holland, Belgium • Forwarded by mail as well as email or by email only, 10 issues per year • Subscription-based service • Subscription Rate: 6 months: US$223/175€; 1 year = US$362/284€; 3 months subscription is also available.

- Songservice.com *http://www.songservice.com*
  Independent A&R and publishing service that enables songwriters to submit songs (a maximum of three songs per songwriter per quarter) to be reviewed and evaluated. Tracks for TV, commercials, and film productions can also be submitted. Should a song be on target, fit a particular request by a client or be deemed as marketable, a publishing contract will be offered to the songwriter. The song will be added to the Songservice catalogue after the contact has been mutually signed • When submitting a song, you will retain your copyright. When signing a publishing agreement, you will, however, agree to split future revenues (currently on a 33/67 basis in favor of the artist, though this can change) from your copyrights in your song with Songservice.com when the song is licensed to users • Publishing contracts have a 5-year term. You will be bound to this contract for this duration. Check which rights you license to them and if the contract is exclusive or non-exclusive • Songservice also acts as mediator between songwriters seeking co-writing partners. Subscription-based • Annual Subscription Rate: US$25 • Service based in the Netherlands, though operates internationally.

- Songquarters *http://www.songquarters.com*
  Swedish Service that provides listings covering Top 500 artists as well as newly signed and developing artists in search of songs • Provides contact directories of the key people working in management, production, publishing, and record companies in numerous counties (excluding Japan, Brazil and Mexico) • Lists leading A&R Managers and Directors and their contact

data • All information is accessible through an online portal with a membership area • Subscription-based service • Subscription Rate: 6 months $225; 1 year: $395 • Genres covered: Dance, Country, Pop, Rock, and Urban.

- Songs Wanted *http://www.songswanted.com*
  German bulletin with listings/leads of artists and bands in search of songs • Forwarded by mail or fax, 10 issues per year • Subscription-based service • Subscription Rate: 6 months: US$97.50/85,54€; 1 year = US$195/165,62€ • Equally provides a 34-page contact directory of German music production companies and A&R managers with their respective domestic artists and/or labels. Updated twice a year. • Cooperates with Songlink International.

- Taxi *http://www.taxi.com*
  Independent A&R service that acts as middleman between their clients (i.e., record companies, publishers, and music supervisors) who are looking for new songs, instrumentals, and tracks for film and TV, and the songwriters who are trying to place their songs in one of these productions. Taxi provides industry listings/leads, reviews and evaluates material submitted to them by songwriters in response to the listings, and forwards the songs to its clients that fit a particular request and reach a certain quality standard set by Taxi. • No contact directory of industry professionals is available to the songwriter • Listings are updated twice a month • Feedback is provided on the material submitted • Taxi also promotes unsigned bands and artists • Subscription-based service • Subscription Rate: 1 year: US$299.95; 2 years: US$499.95; 3 years: US$599.95 • Numerous genres covered.

Find a list of further services marked below (again in no preferential order and with no further comments):

- Hitquarters *http://www.hitquarters.com*
- Song Catalog *http://musicnet.songcatalog.com*
- Song Scope *http://www.songscope.com*
- Songs for sale *http://www.songsforsale.co.uk*
- Sound Taxi *http://www.soundtaxi.net* (royalty-free music)

You may also want to consider contacting a publisher or producer directly to see if there is interest in a collaboration. Picking up the phone and speaking to a representative, PA, or manager in person could end up being worth your while.

Should you be looking further services, check The Music Directory online for further links to interesting sites relating to the music industry.

27
Digital Rights Management

Securing Digital Content ▪ DRM

Securing Digital Content
Digital Rights Management (DRM) is a broadly used term encompassing a number of technologies that allows audio and video material to be encoded and encrypted in order to restrict its usage and thus protect it from illegally being duplicated, sold, and distributed infinitely on the Web. A number of artists, however, maintain that securing digital content and thus protecting their copyrighted material is more a pain than a benefit to them and to their fans and customers who are keen on listening and purchasing their songs. They are not alone in sharing this opinion. Why is this?

The arguments raised by critics point to similar restrictions for users who legally download song files that are encoded with DRM. They assert that their personal use of legal content is equally restricted and that DRM technologies fail to adequately make concessions for fair use. For instance, the number of times copies can be made of a song for private use is limited, as is the number of times a song can be burnt to a CD. DRM also locks the user into using one particular music player, brand of software, or even platform to listen to the encoded files. This has been and currently still is the case. Microsoft's DRM encoded audio and video files in wma/wmv format can only be played on a computer using the proprietary Microsoft Windows Media Player, and RealNetwork's Helix DRM encoded files in real format are bound solely to the Real Media Player on a computer. Apple's iTunes, using several DRM schemes, forces consumers to purchase Apple's proprietary portable music player iPod to listen to songs that have been legally downloaded.

Critics also point to the fact that DRM encryption is not secure, as the underlying algorithms can be broken by downloading and using readily available software from the Web and thus bypassing DRM limitations altogether. The Digital Millennium Copyright Act in the United States, as well as other laws formulated abroad, make it illegal to use systems or software to bypass DRM limitations. Whether this helps to contain the number of illegal copies remains to be seen.

The legal users of DRM encoded files are thus confronted with restrictions in their own usage of downloaded songs next to technological constraints and complications when all they really want is to listen to and enjoy the music. Different technological and proprietary standards are applied by several major players, making it all the more confusing for consumers.

Independent artists and bands are also affected. Deciding on whether or not to use DRM when releasing their songs and where to market and promote their songs may end up being a difficult task. Not all popular online music stores that attract a large number of visitors each day currently support DRM. Those who do not usually offer downloads in mp3 format, a worldwide standard that imposes no restrictions on users, but equally offers no protection for unlimited copying and distribution of such files on the Web or on physical media. So independent artists end up having to assess what is more important to them: the level of exposure to the public or the level of control and security of digital content once their songs are released.

DRM is set up to ensure that only paying consumers can access media and that piracy of copyrighted material is reduced. Piracy has been a huge issue in the recent past leading to declining sales in the music industry, which directly affects artists and songwriters.

Regardless of the methods of distribution selected, a single, platform-independent, though more flexible technological standard would be one step in the right direction. Online music stores should equally give each artist or band the option to decide whether or not they want to distribute DRM-free or DRM-encoded files to the public when releasing their material. Disregarding DRM completely does not really make sense.

More information on the leading companies providing DRM technologies and companies providing DRM solutions is provided below. Also, check The Music Directory online for further links relating to this topic.

DRM Technology Providers
- Microsoft
  http://www.microsoft.com/windows/windowsmedia/forpros/drm/default.mspx
- RealNetworks
  http://www.realnetworks.com/products/drm/index.html
- Macrovision
  http://www.macrovision.com

DRM Solution Providers
- Payplay
  http://www.payplay.com
- Macrovision (equally provides solutions)
  http://www.macrovision.com
- Media Key
  http://www.mediakey.com

28
Music Industry Organizations

BIEM · CISAC · GESAC · IFPI · IFRRO · WIPO

BIEM
Bureau International Des Societes Gérant Les Droits D'Enregistrement et de Reproduction Mécanique. BIEM is the international organization, representing forty-five mechanical rights societies from forty-three countries that administer mechanical rights. BIEM negotiates in the name of its members a standard agreement with IFP fixing the conditions for the use of the repertoire of the societies. BIEM is based in Paris, France, and has two regional offices in Budapest and Singapore. *http://biem.org*

CISAC
CISAC, the International Confederation of Societies of Authors and Composers, works at improving the protection of creators, at enhancing the quality of the collective administration of their rights and at coordinating the activities of authors' societies throughout the world. Through its 210 members in 109 countries, CISAC represents over 2.5 million creators and publishers in every artistic repertoire, including music, audiovisual works, drama, literature, and visual arts. Founded in 1926, CISAC is based in Paris, France, with regional offices in Budapest, Buenos Aires, and Singapore. *http://cisac.org*

GESAC
GESAC represents nearly 500,000 authors or their successors in title in the area of music, graphic and plastic arts, literary and dramatic works, and audiovisual, as well as music publishers. GESAC is a Brussels-based organization working to ensure that the interests of European authors and their collective management societies are heeded by the European institutions. *http://www.gesac.org*

IFPI
IFPI represents the recording industry worldwide with over 1450 members in 75 countries and affiliated Industry associations in 48 countries. IFPI's international Secretariat is based in London and is linked to regional offices in Brussels, Hong Kong, Miami, and

Moscow. IFPI thus represents any company, firm, or person producing sound recordings or music videos which are made available to the public in reasonable quantities. It also acts as an umbrella organization for its national groups and affiliated industry associations. *http://www.ifpi.org*

IFRRO
International Federation of Reproduction Rights Organizations (with 39 member societies worldwide) is an independent organization established to promote the fundamental international copyright principles embodied in the Berne and Universal Copyright Conventions. Its purpose is to facilitate, on an international basis, the collective management of reproduction and other rights relevant to copyrighted works through the co-operation of national Reproduction Rights Organizations (RROs). Collective or centralized rights management is preferable where individual exercise of rights is impractical. *http://www.ifrro.org*

WIPO
The World Intellectual Property Organization is an agency of the United Nations dedicated to promoting the protection of intellectual property on a worldwide basis. WIPO was established by the WIPO Convention in 1967 and is headquartered in Geneva, Switzerland. *http://www.wipo.int*

For more links to music related organizations and associations, check The Music Directory.

29
Moral Rights

Europe ▪ U.K. ▪ U.S.

Europe
The doctrine of moral rights, also called droit moral, was included in the international legal convention of international property, the Berne Convention in 1948, and has now been incorporated into European law. It focuses on protecting the integrity of creative works. The moral rights of a copyrighted musical or literary work are owned by the author of that work. Performers on sound recordings, on the other hand, do not hold such rights.

Moral rights are to be distinguished from copyright. In contrast to copyright, moral rights by law cannot be assigned to another party. Dependent on the national law of a country, it may though be possible for each of the authors to waive their moral rights in a work. Should an author of a work choose to retain his moral rights and at the same time assign his copyright in the work to a third party, he should clearly document this in the publishing contract.

United Kingdom
The Copyright Designs & Patents Act 1988 (CDPA) incorporates four moral rights which are explained in sections 77-89. These are:

1. The right of paternity (which is the right to be properly identified as the author of the work)
2. The integrity right (which is the right not to have an author's work subjected to derogatory treatment)
3. False Attribution (which is the right not to have a work falsely attributed to an author)
4. The right to privacy in any photographs that you commission (which protects against unauthorized use of private photographs that you have commissioned)

The CDPA does nevertheless allow an author to waive his moral rights. This is not common in most of the other European countries.

The first, second, and fourth rights last for the duration of copyright. The third right lasts for twenty years after the author's death. When signing publishing or record label contracts, be sure to check for clauses in which you may be waiving your moral rights.

United States
In the U.S., the legal concept of moral rights for musical works is not recognized. The original authors of numerous songs who live in the U.S. (and in part in the U.K.) and assign their copyright to another party are thus never known.

Any means of protecting the integrity of creative works should therefore be stipulated in the publishing or songwriter contract to be enforced.

Registry of Collecting Societies

Country	Society	PRO	MRS	Full Name	Internet Address	Territories
Albania	ALBAUTOR	x		Société albanaise pour les droits d'auteur et les droits voisins		Albania
Algeria	ONDA	x	x	Office National Des Droits d'Auteur	http://www.onda.dz/	Algeria (N. Africa)
Argentina	SADAIC	x	x	Sociedad Argentina De Autores Y Compositores De Musica	http://www.sadaic.org.ar/	Republic of Argentina
Armenia	ARMAUTHOR	x		ARMAUTHOR NGO		Republic of Armenia
Australia	APRA	x		Australasian Performing Right Association Limited	http://www.apra.com.au/	see page III point A for details
Australia	AMCOS		x	Australasian Mechanical Copyright Owners Society (managed by APRA)	http://www.amcos.com.au/	see page III point A for details
Austria	AKM	x		Autoren, Komponisten Und Musikverleger	http://www.akm.co.at/	Austria
Austria	AUSTRO MECHANA		x	Gesellschaft zur Wahrnehmung mechanisch-musikalischer Urheberrechte GmbH		Austria
Barbados	COSCAP	x		Copyright Society of Composers, Authors and Publishers		Barbados
Belarus	BELAT/CASP	x		Intellectual Property Study and Research Unit		Republic of Belarus
Belgium	SABAM	x	x	Societe Belge Des Auteurs Compositeurs Et Editeurs	http://www.sabam.be/	Belgium
Benin	BUBEDRA	x		Bureau Béninois du Droit d'Auteur		Benin
Brazil	ABRAMUS	x		Copyright Society of Composers, Authors and Publishers Inc.		Brazil
Brazil	UBC	x		União Brasileira de Compositores	http://www.ubc.org.br/	Brazil
Bolivia	SOBODAYCOM	x		Sociedad Boliviana de Autores y Compositores de Musica	http://www.sobodaycom.org/	Bolivia
Bosnia	SQN			Sine Qua Non		Bosnia and Herzegovina
Bulgaria	MUSICAUTOR	x	x	Bulgarian Society Of Authors And Composers For Performing And Mechanical Rights	http://www.musicautor.org/	Bulgaria
Burkina Faso	BBDA			Bureau Burkinabe Du Droit D'auteur		Burkina Faso
Cameroon	SOCINADA/CMC	x		Cameroon Copyright Corporation / Cameroon Music Corporation		Cameroon
Canada	SOCAN	x		Society Of Composers, Authors And Music Publishers Of Canada	http://www.socan.ca/	Canada
Canada	SODRAC		x	Society for Reproduction Rights of Authors, Composers and Publishers in Canada	http://www.sodrac.ca/	Canada
Canada	CMRRA		x	Canadian Musical Reproduction Rights Agency		Canada
Chile	SCD	x	x	Sociedad Chilena Del Derecho De Autor	http://www.scd.cl/	Chile
China	MCSC	x		Music Copyright Society Of China		People's Republic Of China
Central Africa	BUCADA	x		Bureau Centrafricain des Droits d'Auteur		Central African Republic
Colombia	SAYCO	x	x	Sociedad De Autores Y Compositores De Colombia	http://www.sayco.org/	Colombia
Congo	BCDA			Bureau congolais de droits d'auteur		Congo
Congo	SONECA			La société nationale des éditeurs, compositeurs et auteurs de la RDC		Congo
Costa Rica	ACAM	x		Asociacion De Compositores Y Autores Musicales De Costa Rica		Costa Rica
Croatia	HDS	x		Hrvatsko Drustvo Skladatelja Croatian Composers' Society	http://www.sayco.org/	Croatia
Cuba	ACDAM	x		Agencia Cubana de Derecho de Autor Musical	http://www.cuft.cu	Cuba
Czech Rep.	OSA	x	x	Ochranny Svaz Autorsky pro prava k dilum hudebnim	http://www.osa.cz/	Czech Republic
Denmark	KODA	x		Selskabet Til Forvaltning Af Internationale Komponistret-Tigheder - Denmark	http://www.koda.dk/	Denmark, Faroe Isl., Greenland
Denmark	NCB		x	Nordisk Copyright Bureau	http://www.ncb.dk/	see page III point B for details
Dominican Rep.	SGACEDOM	x		Sociedad General de Autores, Compositores y Editores Dominicanos de Musica		Dominican Republic
Ecuador	SAYCE	x		Sociedad de Autores y Compositores Ecuatorianos	http://www.sayce.com.ec/	Ecuador
Egypt	SACERAU	x	x	Société des Auteurs, Compositeurs et Editeurs de la République Arabe d'Egypte		Egypt
Estonia	EAU	x		Eesti Atoritie Uhing	http://www.eauthors.ee/	Estonia

Registry of Collecting Societies

Country	Society	PRO	MRS	Full Name	Internet Address	Territories
Fiji	FCA	x		Fiji Composers Association		Fiji Islands
Finland	TEOSTO	x		Saveltajain Tekijanoikeustoi-Misto	*http://www.teosto.fi/*	Finland
France	SACEM	x		Societe Des Auteurs, Compositeurs Et Editeurs De Musique	*http://www.sacem.fr/*	*see page III point C for details*
France	SDRM		x	Société pour l'administration du Droit de Reproduction Mecanique	*http://www.sdrm.fr*	*see page III point C for details*
Guatemala	AGAYC	x		Asociación Guatemalteca de Autores y Compositores		Guatemala
Georgia	SAS	x		Georgian Society of Authors and Composers		Georgia
Germany	GEMA	x	x	Gesellschaft Für Musikalische Aufführungs-Und Mechanische Vervielfältigungsrechte	*http://www.gema.de/*	Germany
Ghana	COSGA	x		Copyright Society of Ghana		Ghana
Ghana	COPYGHANA	x		Copyright Society of Ghana		Ghana
Greece	AEPI	x	x	Societe Hellenique Pour La Protection De La Propriete Intellectuelle S.A.	*http ://www.aepi.gr/*	Greece
Hong Kong	CASH	x	x	Composers And Authors Society Of Hong Kong Ltd.	*http ://www.cash.org.hk/*	Hong Kong
Hungary	ARTIJUS	x	x	Bureau Hongrois Pour La Protection Des Droits D'auteur	*http ://www.artisjus.hu/*	Hungary
Iceland	STEF	x		Samband Tonskalda Og Egenda Flutningsrettar	*http://www.stef.is/web/*	Iceland
India	IPRS	x		Indian Performing Rights Society	*http://www.indiavibes.com/prs/*	India
Indonesia	KCI	x	x	Yayasan Karya Cipta Indonesia		Indonesia
Ireland	IMRO	x		Irish Music Rights Organisation Limited	*http://www.imro.ie/*	Ireland
Israel	ACUM	x	x	Societe Des Auteurs, Compositeurs Et Editieurs De Musique En Israel	*http ://www.acum.org.il/*	Israel
Italy	IMAIE	x		Institute per la tutela dei diritti degli aristi interpreti esecutori	*http://www.imaie.it*	Italy
Italy	SIAE	x	x	Società Italiana Degli Autori Ed Editori	*http://www.siae.it/*	Italy, Rep. of San Marino, Vatican C.
Ivory Coast	BURIDA	x		Bureau Ivoirien du Droit d'Auteur	*http://www.mcf-culture.ci/fr/ministere/*	Ivory Coast
Jamaica	JACAP	x		Jamaica Association of Composers, Authors and Publishers Ltd.	*http://www.jipo.gov.jm/*	Jamaica
Japan	JASRAC	x	x	Japanese Society For Rights Of Authors, Composers And Publishers	*http://www.jasrac.or.jp/ejhp/*	Japan
Kazakhstan	KAZAK	x		Kazakhstan Authors Society		Kazakhstan Republic
Kenya	MCSK	x	x	Music Copyright Society of Kenya	*http://www.mcsk.or.ke*	Kenya
Korea	KOMCA	x	x	Korea Music Copyright Association (South Korea)		Republic Of Korea (South Korea)
Latvia	AKKA/LAA	x		Copyright And Communication Consulting Agency/Latvian Copyright Agency	*https://www.akka-laa.lv/*	Latvia
Lithuania	LATGA-A			Agency Of Lithuanian Copyright Protection Association	*http://www.latga.lt/*	Republic Of Lithuania
Macedonia	ZAMP	x		Musical Copyright Society	*http://www.hds.hr/*	Former Yogo Rep. of Macedonia
Madagascar	OMDA	x	x	Office Malgache des Droits d'Auteur	*http://www.omda.mg/*	Madagascar
Malawi	COSOMA	x	x	Copyright Society of Malawi	*http://www.cosoma.org/*	Malawi
Malaysia	MACP	x		Music Authors' Copyright Protection Berhad	*http://www.macp.com.my/*	Malaysia
Mauritius	MASA	x		Mauritius Society of Authors	*http://www.masa.mu*	Mauritius
Morocco	BMDA	x	x	Le Bureau marocain du droit d'auteur	*http://www.bmda.org.ma/*	Morocco
Mexico	SACM	x	x	Sociedad De Autores Y Compositores De Musica. S. De A.	*http://www.sacm.org.mx/*	Mexico
Namibia	NASCAM	x		Namibian Society of Composers and Authors of Music		Namibia
Nepal	CPSN	x		Copyright Protection Society of Nepal		Nepal
Netherlands	BUMA	x		Vereniging Buma auteursrecht-organ. van componisten, tekstdicht en muziekuitgevers	*http://www.bumastemra.nl*	*see page III point D for details*
Netherlands	STEMRA		x	Stichting Stemra	*http://www.bumastemra.nl*	*see page III point D for details*
New Zealand	APRA	x		Australasian Performing Right Association Limited	*http://www.apra.com.au/*	*see page III point A for details*
New Zealand	AMCOS		x	Australasian Mechanical Copyright Owners Society (managed by APRA)	*http://www.amcos.com.au/*	*see page III point A for details*
Nigeria	MCSN		x	Musical Copyright Society of Nigeria		Nigeria
Norway	TONO	x		Norsk Komponistforenings Internasjonale Musikkbyra	*http://www.tono.no/*	Bear + Hope + Jan Mayen Island, Norway, Spitsbergen

Country	Society	PRO	MRS	Full Name	Internet Address	Territories
Panama	SPAC	x				Panama
Paraguay	APA	x				Paraguay
Peru	APDAYC	x		Asociacion Peruana De Autores Y Compositores		Peru
Philippines	FILSCAP	x		Filipino Society Of Composers, Authors And Publishers, Inc.		Philippine Republic
Poland	ZAIKS	x	x	Stowarzyszenie Autorow	http://www.zaiks.org.pl/	Poland
Polynesia	SPACEM			The French Polynesia Society of Artists , Composers and Music Publishers	http://www.spc.org.nc/culture/	Polynesia
Portugal	SPA	x	x	Sociedade Portuguesa De Autores	http://www.spautores.pt/	Azores, Madeira, Portugal
Rep. of Guinea	BGDA	x		Bureau Guinéen des Droits d'Auteur		Republic of Guinea
Republic of Mali	BUMDA			Bureau Malien du Droit d'Auteur	http://www.bumda.cefib.com	Republic of Mali
Romania	UCMR-ADA	x	x	Union Of Composers And Musicologists In Romania/ Authors' Right Department		Romania
Russia	RAO	x		Russian Authors Society	http://www.rao.ru/	Russian Federation
Senegal	BSDA	x		Bureau Sénégalais du droit d'auteur		Senegal
Serbia & Montenegro	SOKOJ	x	x	Savez Organizacija Kompozitora Jugoslavije	http://www.sokoj.org.yu/	Serbia & Montenegro
Slovak Republic	SOZA	x	x	Slovensky Ochranny Zvaz Autorsky / Slovak Performing and Mechanical Rights Society	http://www.soza.sk	Slovak Republic
Slovenia	SAZAS	x	x	Société Des Compositeurs, Auteurs Et Editeurs De Slovenie	http://www.sazas.org	Slovenia
Singapore	COMPASS		x	Composers And Authors Society Of Singapore Ltd	http://www.compass.org.sg/	Singapore
South Africa	SAMRO	x		Southern African Music Rights Organisation Limited	http://www.samro.org.za	see page III point F for details
South Africa	SARRAL		x	South Africa Recording Rights Association		South Africa
Spain	SGAE	x		Sociedad General De Autores De Espana	http ://www.sgae.es/	Spain
Sri Lanka	SLPRS	x		Sri Lanka Performing Right Society		Sri Lanka
Sweden	STIM	x		Svenska Tonsattares Internationella Musikbyra	http://www.stim.se/	Sweden
Switzerland	SUISA	x	x	Schweizerische Gesellschaft für die Rechte der Urheber musikalischer Werke	http://www.suisa.ch/	Liechtenstein, Switzerland
Taiwan	CHA	x		Copyright Holder's Association, Chinese Taipei (Taiwan)		Taiwan
Taiwan	MUST	x		Music Copyright Intermediary Society Of Chinese Taipei		Taiwan, Republic of China
Thailand	MCT	x		Music Copyright Thailand Limited		Thailand
Togo	BUTODRA	x		Bureau Togolais du Droit d'Auteur	http://www.butodra.org/	Togo
Trinidad & Tobago	COTT	x	x	Copyright Organisation of Trinidad and Tobago	http://www.tidco.co.tt/local/cott/cott.htm	Trinidad & Tobago
Tunisia						Tunisia
Turkey	MESAM	x	x	Turkiye Musiki Eseri Sahipleri Mesiek Birligi	http://www.mesam.org.tr	Turkey
Ukraine	UACRR/SCAU	x		Ukrainian Agency of Copyright and Related Rights		Ukraine
United Kingdom	PRS	x		The Performing Rights Society Ltd.	http://www.prs.co.uk/	see page III point G for details
United Kingdom	MCPS		x	Mechanical-Copyright Protection Society Ltd	http://www.mcps.co.uk/	see page III point G for details
Uruguay	AGADU	x	x	Asociacion General De Autores Del Uruguay	http://www.agadu.com/	Uruguay
USA	ASCAP	x		The American Society of Composers, Authors and Publishers	http://www.ascap.com/	USA
USA	BMI	x		Broadcast Music, Inc.	http://www.bmi.com/	USA
USA	SESAC	x		SESAC (formerly known as Society of European Stage Authors & Composers)	http://www.sesac.com	USA
USA	HFA		x	Harry Fox Agency, Inc.	http://www.hfa.com/	USA
Venezuela	SACVEN	x		Sociedad De Autores Y Compositores De Venezuela	http ://www.sacven.org	Venezuela
Zaire	SONECA			Societe Nationale Des Editeurs, Compositeurs Et Auteurs		Zaire
Zambia	ZAMCOPS		x	Zambia Music Copyright Protection Society		Zambia
Zimbabwe	ZIMRA	x		Zimbabwe Music Rights Association		Zimbabwe

PRO = Performance Rights Society   **MRS = Mechanical Rights Society**

This list does not contain all rights societies.

Collecting Societies Territorial Administration

A The Australasian Performing Right Association Limited (**APRA**) administers the rights for the following territories:

Ashmore Island, Australia, Australian Antarctic Territory, Cartier Island, Christmas Islands, Cocos (Keeling) Islands, Cook, Fiji Islands, Heard Islands, Kiribati, Macquarie Island, Mcdonald Island, Nauru, New Zealand, Niue (Savage) Island, Norfolk Island, Papua-New Guinea, Ross Dependency, Solomon Islands, Tokelau (Union) Islands, Tuvalu, Western Samoa.

B The Nordisk Copyright Bureau (**NCB**) administers mechanical rights for the following territories:

Denmark, Estonia, Finland, Iceland, Latvia, Lithuania, Norway, Sweden, Faroe Islands

C The Societe Des Auteurs, Compositeurs Et Editeurs De Musique (**SACEM**) and the Société pour l'administration du Droit de Reproduction Mécanique (**SDRM**) administer the rights for the following territories :

French Republic & its overseas departments (Guadeloupe, Guyane, Martinique, Reunion), Polynesia, Wallis & Futuna, New Caledonia, Mayotte, Saint-Pierre & Miquelon, French Austral and Antartic territories (TAAF), B. Luxemburg, Monaco1orra, Lebanon. Benin (BUBEDRA), Burkina Faso (BBDA), Cameroon, Central African Rep. (BUCADA), Congo (BCDA), Ivory Coast (BURIDA), Egypt (SACERAU), Guinea (BGDA), Madagascar (OMDA), Mali (BUMDA), Morocco (BMDA), Niger (BNDA), Senegal (BSDA), Togo (BUTODRA).

D The Vereniging Buma (**BUMA**) and Stichting **STEMRA** administer the rights for following territories:

The Netherlands, Netherlands Antilles: Aruba, Bonaire, Curaçao, Saba, St. Eustatius, St. Martin, Surinam Indonesia: Borneo (Kalimantan), Celebs, Moluccas, Sunda Isles, Irian Barat

E The Performing Rights Society Ltd. (**PRS**) administers the following territories:

Anguilla, Antigua, Ascension Island, Bahamas, Bangladesh, Barbuda, Belize, Bermuda, British Antarctic Territory, British Indian Ocean Territory, British Virgin Islands, Brunei, Cayman Islands, Channel Islands, Cyprus, Diego Garcia, Dominica, Falkland Islands, Ghana, Gibraltar, Grenada, Guyana, Kenya, Malawi, Malta, Man (Isle Of), Monserrat, Nigeria, Pakistan, Pitcairn Islands, Seychelles, Sierra Leone, South Georgia, South Sandwich Islands, Sri Lanka, St. Helena, St. Kitts-Nevis, St. Lucia, St. Vincent, Tanzania, Tonga, Tristan Da Cunha, Turks And Caicos Islands, Uganda, United Kingdom, Zambia, Zimbabwe

F The Southern African Music Rights Organisation Limited (**SAMRO**) administers the following territories:

Botswana, Lesotho, Republic Of South Africa (Including Bophuthatswana And Transkei) South-West Africa, Swaziland.

G The Mechanical-Copyright Protection Society Ltd. (**MCPS**) administers mechanical rights for the following territories:

United Kingdom & The British Commonwealth (excluding Australasia, Canada, the Gambia, Botswana, Lasotho and Swaziland), Anguilla, Antigua & Barbuda, Bahamas, Bangladesh, Barbados (COSCAP), Belize, Bermuda, British Antarctic Territory, British Indian Ocean Territory, British Virgin Islands, Brunei, Cayman Islands, Cyprus, Dominica, Falkland Islands, Ghana, Gibraltar, Grenada, Guyana, India (IPRS), Ireland (republic of) - through MCPS Ireland, Jamaica (JACAP), Kenya, Malawi, Malaysia (MACP).

Index

Further Reading

The following books may also be of interest to you:

Avalon, Moses, *Secrets of Negotiating a Record Contract*, Backbeat Books, 2001, ISBN 0-87930-636-X (focuses primarily on the U.S. market)

Krasilovski, M. William and Shemel, Sydney, *The Business of Music*, Billboard Books, 2003, ISBN 0-8230-7728-4 (focuses primarily on the U.S. market)

Lyng, Robert, Musik & Moneten, PPV Medien, 2001, ISBN 3-932275-24-1 (focuses primarily on the German market; published in German)

Music Managers Forum, *The Music Management Bible*, Sanctuary Publishing, 2003, ISBN 1-84492-025-9 (focuses primarily on the U.K. market)

Passman, Donald S., *All You Need to Know About the Music Business*, Simon & Schuster, 2003, ISBN 0-684-87064-9 (focuses primarily on the U.S. market)

About the Author

Henri Biermans is a graduate from CIG in Switzerland and Boston University with a major in Finance. He worked in the financial services industry for several years. He then decided to focus on the music business with the attempt to make a dream come true: composing and producing music. The information in this book covers important details he picked up over the last few years while setting up and running his business. He lives near London in the United Kingdom.

[1] Performer's rights from U.K. Patent Office. http://www.patent.gov.uk/copy/indetail/performers.htm. Retrieved June 20 2006

[2] Data extrapolated from contracts inspected by Musicians Union. http://ww.musiciansunion.org.uk

[3] Publishing from Wikipedia. http://en.wikipedia.org/wiki/Publisher. Retrieved July 18 2006

[4] Mechanical Rights from BIEM http://www.biem.org/. Retrieved July 19 2006

[5] BIEM FAQ. http://www.biem.org/content.aspx?MenuItemId=5. Retrieved July 19 2006

[6] Dart Factsheet from U.S. Copyright Office. http://www.copyright.gov/carp/dartfact.html

[7] Blank Media Levies from Wikipedia. http://en.wikipedia.org/wiki/Blank_media_tax

[8] Record Rental Amendment of 1984, Pub. L. No. 98-450, 98 Stat. 1727 (amending §109 and §115, title 17, U.S.C)

[9] Council Directive 92/100/EEC. http://eur-lex.europa.eu/LexUriServ/LexUriServ.do?uri=CELEX:31992L0100:EN:HTML

[10] The Directorate General Communication. http://europa.eu.int, Reference: IP/04/891.

[11] BMI Licensing Options from BMI. http://www.bmi.com/licensing/webcaster/webfaq.asp

[12] PPL. http://www.ppluk.com/

[13] SoundExchange. http://www.soundexchange.com/faq.html. Retrieved Sep. 6 2006

[14] 2005 RIAA yrEndStats

[15] Copyright Registration of MC and SR from U.S. Copyright Office. http://www.copyright.gov/register/pa-sr.html. Retrieved Aug. 2006

[16] Circular 50 from U.S. Copyright Office. http://www.copyright.gov/circs/circ50.pdf. Retrieved Aug. 2006

[17] Forms of Notice from the U.S. Copyright Office. http://www.copyright.gov/circs/. Retrieved June 20 2006

[18] Definition of Cover Version. http://en.wikipedia.org/wiki/Cover_version. Retrieved August 3 2006

[19] *Brand* from Wikipedia. http://en.wikipedia.org/wiki/Brand. Retrieved May 25 2006

[20] *Record label* from Wikipedia. http://en.wikipedia.org/wiki/Record_label. Retrieved May 25 2006

[21] *What is a trademark* from USPTO. http://www.uspto.gov/web/offices/tac/tmfaq.htm

[22] *Do you have a 800 number* from USPTO. http://www.uspto.gov/main/faq/index.html. June 2 2006

[23] ISRC Handbook. http://www.ifpi.org/isrc/isrc_handbook.html#Heading140. Retrieved Aug 31 2006

[24] *ICANN Information* from ICANN. http://www.icann.org/general/. Retrieved May 29 2006

[25] *FAQs* from InterNic. http://www.internic.net/faqs/domain-names.html. Retrieved May 29 2006

[26] IFPI Press release (Digital formats continue to ...). http://www.ifpi.org/site-content/press/20060331a.html

[27] Digital Music Report 2006 by IFPI. http://www.ifpi.org/site-content/press/20060119.html

[28] RIAA 2005yrEndStats. http://www.riaa.com/news/newsletter/pdf/2005yrEndStats.pdf

[29] IAA: Music Sales Resume Decline In '05 By Joseph Palenchar/TWICE. April 10 2006 (modified accordingly)

[30] NPD Press Release from NPD Group. http://npd.com/dynamic/releases/press_051121a.html

[31] RIAA About us. http://www.riaa.com/about/default.asp

Printed in the United States
113844LV00001B/18/A

9 780955 568008